T0166178

Calling and Vocation

For the Social Sciences Institute (SI) of the
Evangelical Church in Germany (EKD).
With Contributions by Gerhard Wegner,
Anika Füser and Gunther Schendel

Gunther Schendel (ed.)
Translated by Ray Cunningham

Calling and Vocation

From Martin Luther to the

Modern World of Work

EVANGELISCHE VERLAGSANSTALT
Leipzig

Bibliographic information published by the German National Library
The Deutsche Nationalbibliothek lists this publication in the Deutsche
Nationalbiographie; detailed bibliographic data are available on the
Internet at http://dnb.dnb.de

This book was printed on FSC-certified paper.

Cover: Kai-Michael Gustmann, Leipzig with support by creo-media.de
Lectorate: Gabriele Arndt-Sandrock/Gunther Schendel
Typesetting: Formenorm, Friederike Arndt, Leipzig
Printing and Binding: Hubert & Co., Göttingen

ISBN 978-3-374-05225-7
www.eva-leipzig.de

Content

Introduction: Much more than just an activity 7
Gunther Schendel

Vocation – History and presence of a revolution . . 25
Gerhard Wegner

»God at Work« or, What Workplace
Spirituality has to say about vocation 67
Gunther Schendel

»My work is the meaning in my life«:
Portrait pages presenting people in very different
occupations . . . . dispersed throughout the volume
Anika Füser

Abbreviations. 101

The Authors 102

Introduction: Much more than just an activity

Gunther Schendel

1. Vocation and calling today

»Vocations« is the title of a weekly column in the New York Times. The motto for this column is »People from all walks of life talk about their jobs«.[1] So every week a different person is visited at their workplace and asked a series of questions. »An Ethnographer of Cancer Care« is a researcher – a sculptor with a degree in fine arts – who is studying doctor-patient communications in the treatment of cancer for a medical software firm.[2] The »Treehouse Builder« is a carpenter who graduated from a vocational-technical high school and for several years now has been building treehouses in oak and maple treetops. The best thing about it, he says, is climbing without ladders.[3] »A Women's Advocate Who's Passionate About Progress«: this is a woman with a degree in politics and communications who is now responsible for a women's initiative at the charitable foundation established by a former US President. Her focus is on access to education, health care and income opportunities for disadvantaged women. It is the contact with First Ladies that she finds particularly inspiring – and what

---

1   https://www.nytimes.com/column/vocations (accessed: 8.5.2017).

2   Patricia A. Olsen, An Ethnographer of Cancer Care, New York Times, Feb. 24, 2017, online: https://www.nytimes.com/2017/02/24/jobs/watson-health-cancer-ibm-design-researcher.html?_r=0 (accessed: 8.5.2017).

3   Patricia A. Olsen, A Treehouse Builder Who's Having a Ball in the Branches, New York Times, Dec. 9, 2016, online: https://www.nytimes.com/2016/12/09/jobs/a-treehouse-builder-whos-having-a-ball-in-the-branches.html (accessed: 8.5.2017).

these women, with their experience and their passion, can do for others.[4]

What is appealing about this column is the breadth and diversity of the occupations depicted there. But there is something else that makes this column interesting, and that is that the men and women it showcases certainly don't see their work as just another job. Their work is more. It is linked to their inclinations and interests. It sometimes has its roots in their biographies, although their formal education and training has not necessarily led them directly to it; biographical ruptures and changes of direction often play a role. And finally: their work brings them fulfilment – the feeling of doing something meaningful.

So these columns are about work *and* the meaning or purpose of work. This reflects the ambiguity in the title »Vocations« – which in terms of semantic breadth is roughly comparable with the German terms »Beruf« and »Berufung«. Vocations: these are the specific occupations which can be included in a »list of vocations« and to which a specific »vocational education« can lead. But the word »vocation« can also indicate subjectivity: vocation as »a strong feeling of suitability for a particular career or occupation«.[5] And its meaning can extend still further, up to and including »a divine call to the religious life«.[6] It is no coincidence that the offices maintained by some Roman Catholic dioceses in the USA for the recruitment of the next generation of priests are

4   Patricia A. Olsen, A Women's Advocate Who's Passionate About Progress, New York Times, Dec. 3, 2016, online: https://www.nytimes.com/2016/12/03/jobs/a-womens-advocate-whos-passionate-about-progress.html (accessed: 8.5.2017).

5   English Oxford living Dictionaries, »Vocation«, online: https://en.oxforddictionaries.com/definition/vocation (accessed: 8.5.2017).

6   Merriam Webster, »Vocation«, online: https://www.merriam-webster.com/dictionary/vocation (accessed: 8.5.2017).

called »Vocation Offices«.[7] And two Protestant writers speak of »Family Vocation«, of »God's Calling in Marriage, Parenting, and Childhood«.[8]

So the keyword »vocation« opens up a broad semantic field, as does the related word »calling«. Bryan J. Dik and Ryan D. Duffy, two US occupational psychologists, have tried to bring together and summarise the two terms »vocation« and »calling« in one concept.[9] According to them, »vocation« is characterised by (1.) an overarching focus on meaningfulness, and (2.) an orientation towards others (connecting work to »an overall sense of meaning toward other-oriented ends«), whereas »calling« involves a third dimension, namely an external motivation for the activity, regardless of the precise external source (»such as God, a family legacy, or a pressing societal need«).

---

7   Homepage of the ARCHDIOCESE OF NEW YORK, https://archny.org/vocation-office (accessed: 8.5.2017).

8   GENE EDWARD VEITH JR./ MARY J. MOERBE, Family Vocation: God's Calling in Marriage, Parenting, and Childhood, Wheaton, Illinois 2012.

9   BRYAN J. DIK/RYAN D. DUFFY, Calling and Vocation in Career Counseling. Recommendations for Promoting Meaningful Work, Professional Psychology: Research and Practice, in: Professional Psychology: Research and Practice 2009, Vol. 40, No. 6, 625–632 (online: https://www.researchgate.net/publication/232505560_Calling_and_Vocation_in_Career_Counseling_Recommendations_for_Promoting_Meaningful_Work [accessed: 8.5.2017]).

The three dimensions of calling und vocation according to Dik and Duffy

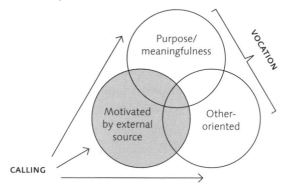

(graphic created by the author)

The three dimensions identified by these two occupational psychologists are helpful because they underline once more that vocation and calling can refer to »much more than just an activity«. The expectation and the experience of meaningfulness, socio-ethical and theological factors can all play a role as well.

Even if talk of the secularisation of vocation is now more than commonplace (and rightly so!)[10], the search for the subjective meaning of work, and thus also for the religious/spiritual and socio-ethical meaning of vocation, is unquestionably worthwhile. This is evidenced by the contributions to this book, which are concerned with precisely these dimensions of the meaning of vocation. The first of these contributions focuses on the concept of vocation as developed by the Reformer Martin Luther, in which faith, secular engagement and serving one's neighbour are

---

10 Douglas J. Schuurman, Vocation: Discerning Our Callings in Life, Grand Rapids 2004, 1–3, and: Falk Wagner, Art. Berufung III. Dogmatisch, in: TRE, Vol. 5, Berlin / New York 1980, 692.

bound strongly together. This contribution traces the long history of the influence of this concept both within and without the Protestant churches up to the present day. It concludes with the urgent question of how to organise the world of work today in such a way that those engaged in it can still (or once again) carry out their activities as a form of vocation, in the fulfilment of their communicative capabilities.

The second contribution is on Workplace Spirituality, which is particularly widespread in the English-speaking world. In the USA, especially, it has in recent years taken on the form of a movement open to very different religious and spiritual influences. This contribution presents by way of example several Protestant concepts as well as one which is more »fluid« in terms of content, and not shaped by a specific religion. The discussion of these concepts leads to the identification of criteria for a discourse of vocation/calling that would be relevant to contemporary life.

In addition, a number of portrait pages are dispersed throughout the volume in which – much like in the »Vocations« series – people in very different occupations tell us about how they relate to their work. These interviews were conducted in northern Germany, and they underline once more the enormous importance of work for the individual's self-perception. »My work is an important part of my life«, says one of the interviewees, a lawyer working for an insurance company. And a woman training to be a physiotherapist emphasises the point: »I believe my work is the meaning in my life«.

2. The background: the renaissance of vocation and the question of meaning

And indeed, the theme that recurs, more or less explicitly, throughout the interviews and other contributions to this book is the question of meaning in work. Whether the topic is theological interpretation, ethical standards or ideas of how to achieve fulfilment through work – the background is always given by certain expectations and experiences of meaningfulness associated with work. For this reason, it is worthwhile at this point to delve further into the question of meaningfulness (and thus also into the ambivalence of certain expectations of meaningfulness).

My theory with regard to this question is that it is precisely this search for meaning in work which has led to the contemporary renaissance in the discourse on vocation. The Workplace Spirituality movement mentioned above, and also the many career guidance services available which explicitly refer to vocations or callings, provide evidence for the existence of such a renaissance of vocation. A writer in Forbes magazine describes »20 Ways to Find Your Calling«[11]; and a professionally produced web page with the title »Find your calling« promises to help young people with their career search.[12] In Germany, a self-appointed »Vocation Consultant« offers his services on the Internet, and visitors to his homepage are posed the classic questions, »What are you on fire for? What makes your heart sing? What really interests you? What are your predilections? «[13] Another »Vocational Consultancy« wants to know »What makes you unique – what is your real essence?«

The unspoken assumption here is that a vocation is more than a job: it involves finding a certain fit between the person and the occupation, whether for someone just setting out on their career path or their education or training, or moving into self-employ-

---

11 JESSICA HAGY, 20 Ways to Find Your Calling, Forbes Magazine, Jun. 26, 2012, online: https://www.forbes.com/sites/jessicahagy/2012/06/26/20-ways-to-find-your-calling/#2d8bfb6f5b7d (accessed: 8.5.2017).

12 https://www.findyourcalling.com/ (accessed: 8.5.2017).

13 THOMAS MALBURG, BerufungsBerater, 2011, online: http://www.derberufungs-berater.de/infos/index.php (accessed: 8.5.2017).

ment, or contemplating a change of career direction or even a mid-life career switch, or for someone contemplating pursuing »vocation instead of retirement«.[14] A similar assumption lies behind the numerous printed vocational guides available, to which the German sociologist Dirk Kaesler devoted a study several years ago. The wide circulation enjoyed by these guides is shown by the fact that a student of Kaesler's conducting internet research found about 2,000 such titles listed on a major online sales platform.[15]

Where does this great interest in vocation come from? Kaesler takes a close look at the situation in Germany, and suggests a link between this interest and a »prevailing sense of uncertainty over career choices«. On the one hand, a great many career opportunities are opening up (assuming formal education or training has been completed); on the other hand, their future viability is often difficult to judge. Therefore taking into account one's own vocation, that is, the »›endogenous‹ (i.e. internal, individual) [...] factors«, would appear to be a very useful aid to decision-making.[16]

The interest in finding a meaningful occupation is correspondingly high, especially among adolescents and young adults. Evidence for this comes from German surveys, but also from international ones. As long ago as 2006, the Shell Youth Study showed that the majority of young people in Germany (»with the possible exception of those with a materialistic orientation«) »pursued their careers motivated not by financial considerations but in fact by an ambitious concept of self-realisation, creativity

---

14   WULF-PETER PAEZOLD, Berufungsberatung, 2013, online: http://www.berufungsberatung.de/angebot/berufungsberatung (accessed: 8.5.2017).

15   DIRK KAESLER, Wie finde ich meine Berufung? Warum es immer noch besser ist, Max Weber zu lesen als Tarot-Karten zu legen, in: literaturkritik.de, September 2011, http://literaturkritik.de/id/15890 (accessed: 8.5.2017).

16   Ibid.

Alexander

self-employed hairdresser
with his own salon

»My work means everything to me, it's my life, because it satisfies my heart and my soul. I can do the thing that I really like doing. For me, my work is a vocation. Every day that I can spend here is a pleasure. So I couldn't imagine anything else. It really is very fulfilling for me.

I come from a family of hairdressers, and I'm the second generation now. It's something I was born into. And I was never very interested in school and always wanted to do some kind of trade or craft. So I started my apprenticeship at 15. I love my job, I love hair, and I never get tired of it.

I love it especially over the Christmas period. Because although people are stressed, they really relax at the hairdresser's. Everyone wants to look good for Christmas, so for us it really is the main time of the year. There's a special atmosphere then. I always enjoy wishing people a ›Merry Christmas‹.

What I don't like at work is staff who need to be trained up, and who can be the cause of lots of complaints. Of course, when you have staff, you have problems. And there are crisis times when, as a boss, you hold your hands to your head and say, ›How am I going to survive to the end of this month?‹ I started my own business at 22, that's really young. But as time goes on you learn to take it easy.

If money didn't come into it, I would still remain a hairdresser. I love this job so much that I would still continue working as a hairdresser even if I won the lottery. I couldn't imagine anything else.

I hope that I stay healthy for a long, long time and that my business remains successful. And that I continue to really enjoy my work.«

and meaningfulness«.[17] These findings are supported by the most recent Study in 2015: 90 percent of the young people between 12 and 25 surveyed want their work to provide them with »the opportunity to do something that has meaning and purpose for me«, and 85 percent hope to have »a chance to do something socially useful«. These aims are in third and fifth place respectively for young people, whereas good prospects for advancement and high earnings lie only in seventh and eighth place (78 and 77 percent). The most important considerations for these young people are security of employment and the opportunity to put forward their own ideas (95 and 93 percent respectively).[18]

So the expectation that work should provide meaning and purpose is widespread; this is also confirmed by the results of international surveys among students and other representatives of the well-educated and internet-savvy Generation Y, aka the »Millennials«.[19] According to a recent survey of 240,000 business and engineering students carried out by an international employer branding firm among others, most of them »want two things in their career: a sense of purpose and the ability to innovate«.[20] Similar results emerged from a survey among Millennials already embarked on their careers in large private com-

17 Klaus Hurrelmann, Lebenssituation und Wertorientierungen der jungen Generation. Ergebnisse der 15. Shell Jugendstudie, [um 2007], 10, online: http://www.uni-bielefeld.de/gesundhw/ag4/downloads/shell15.pdf (accessed: 8.5.2017).

18 Ingo Leven/Gudrun Quenzel/Klaus Hurrelmann, Familie, Bildung, Beruf, Zukunft: Am liebsten alles, in: Mathias Albert et al: Jugend 2015, 17. SHELL Jugendstudie, Frankfurt a. M. 2015, 79.

19 Both terms are often used synonymously. The generation of the Millennials is people who were born in the 1990s. (The current Deloitte Millennial Survey includes people born after 1982 [The 2017 Deloitte Millennial Survey, 2017, 2, online: https://www2.deloitte.com/global/en/pages/about-deloitte/articles/millennialsurvey.html; accessed: 8.5.2017]).

20 Julie Verhage, The Companies where the Millennials want to work the most, Bloomberg, 24. Juni 2015, online: https://www.bloomberg.com/news/articles/2015-06-24/the-companies-where-millennials-want-to-work-the-most (accessed: 8.5.2017).

panies across 30 countries. The Deloitte Millennial Survey 2017 revealed that many respondents see their job as the place where they can achieve most; a place »that contrasts, perhaps, with the less stable world that exists outside the workplace«.[21] In their own estimation, they can exert little influence on many major social problems; but at work they can feel themselves to be »an active participant rather than a bystander«.[22]

These findings confirm the importance of *self-managed* or *autonomous* working as a source of meaningfulness.[23] At least, this certainly applies to the well-educated »digital natives«, »who are used to forging their own path«.[24] But it seems that their expectations are constrained by external limits: some 51 percent of graduates in the USA feel »underemployed«, and small firms and even startups can be more attractive as an employer than a large, prestigious firm in which individual employees are more or less invisible.[25]

This brings us to the downside of the high expectations of meaningfulness placed on work, namely the not uncommon experience of meaninglessness, or at least of a deficit of meaning, at the workplace. In the traditional discourse on alienation at work, such experiences are often associated with a Fordist, assembly-

---

21   2017 Deloitte Millennial Survey (see note 19), 15.

22   Ibid., 13. The influence observed here is fragmentary and does not apply to »leaders or big issues«. Rather, it concerns their peers, customers, and suppliers.

23   A certain proximity to the New Work Movement (NWM) arises here, cf. the interview with Frithjof Bergmann, a leading figure of NWM who explicitly refers to the concept of Calling (»Vollbeschäftigung ist lächerlich«, in: The European, 14.10.2013, online: http://www.theeuropean.de/frithjof-bergmann/7353-alte-denkmuster-und-neue-arbeitskultur [accessed: 8.5.2017]). For a critique of this concept see Lars Vollmer, Denkfehler der New-Work-Bewegung, Capital, 24. Sep. 2016, online: http://www.capital.de/meinungen/der-denkfehler-der-new-work-bewegung.html).

24   Tanya Pinto, Millenials want a sense of purpose at work, in: peakon, Jul. 14th, 2016, online: https://peakon.com/blog/post/millennials-want-a-sense-of-purpose-at-work (accessed: 8.5.2017).

25   Ibid.

line working environment.[26] However, even highly-qualified employees working in professional services are not safe from such experiences. This is confirmed in a recent German study of doctors and social workers. These are employees in positions of authority, who certainly enjoy a degree of decision-making autonomy and managerial responsibility. Despite this, they too experience »a loss of meaning and purpose in their work«, as the interviews conducted for this study show.[27] A decisive contributory factor in this are the tensions arising in work procedures because of contemporary processes of work intensification. Employees see themselves as caught in a constant »balancing act« between work and private life, between an expectation of »meaningful content in work« and concerns for their own »capacity for work«.[28] At the same time, they have to reach decisions on »the relative importance of different competing tasks«, all the while unable to carry out their work »properly«, i.e. to meet their own standards. And this is combined with the experience of losing »positive experiential spaces« such as the »lunch break«.[29]

But another thing which is remarkable about this study is the references it makes to »resources of meaningfulness«. The writer Friedericke Hardering points to a three-fold benefit in terms of meaningfulness which employees derive from their labour:

1. the »benefit of the outcome for themselves«, and the associated feelings of »pride and self-efficacy«.
2. the »benefit of progress with regard to the thing itself«; this refers to furthering »what is socially desirable«.

---

26 Cf. FRIEDERICKE HARDERING, Wann erleben Beschäftigte ihre Arbeit als sinnvoll? Befunde aus einer Untersuchung über professionelle Dienstleistungsarbeit, Zeitschrift für Soziologie, Vol. 46/1 (Feb. 2017), 39.

27 Ibid., 45.

28 Ibid.

29 Ibid.

3. the »benefit of the outcome for others«, and the associated »recognition«.[30]

Hardering speaks of three »experiential sources of meaningful work«[31], and, remarkably, these sources are not very far away from the dimensions of vocation and calling identified at the beginning of this text. The social benefit, and the universally observable orientation towards meaningfulness, recall the definition given for »vocation«, while the external motivation characteristic for »calling« can be more readily seen in the orientation towards progress. According to the study, it is measured by »external yardsticks« such as »health, personal development, social progress and quality of life«.[32] But it is not only these individual factors which are important in providing a sense of meaning or purpose, but also and especially the interaction between them. Whereas a sense of meaninglessness is associated with tension and conflicts, a sense of meaningfulness or purpose at work is associated with »congruence and consistency«.[33] Such positive experiences then represent an important resource for coping with stress and work intensification[34], this perspective therefore also certainly helps to explain the desire among many adolescents and young adults to find work which is meaningful.

It is nevertheless open to question whether placing one's hopes exclusively on one's career as a source of meaningfulness is likely to be successful. The German writer Mercedes Lauenstein warns against the pressure that can be created by the search for »a truly fulfilling career«. Her focus is on Generation Y, whose

---

30   Ibid., 50.
31   Ibid.
32   Ibid., 48.
33   Ibid., 50.
34   Ibid., 52.

members would much prefer »not to march like lemmings into the office« and »not to have to do standard mainstream jobs«. »It is harder to find happiness«, she writes, »than it is to single-mindedly work your way up the career ladder«. And the »wish for a ›fulfilling life‹« brings with it »a much nastier form of performance pressure«.[35]

Such questioning is nothing new; it brings to mind the debate around what was called the »tyranny of happiness«[36], which of course is a side effect of the individualism of late modernity with its pressure towards self-optimisation. What is becoming clear is the ambivalent relationship between our desire for meaningfulness and happiness and the world of work: our expectations in this regard are absolutely understandable, but they can become a binding constriction which merely serves to further increase the pressure on the individual. One of the tasks of a proper Protestant perspective is that of relativizing this expectation, which has a solid basis in theology. This is why the Council of the Evangelical Church in Germany outlined the significance of work as follows in a Memorandum of 2015: »Even as work is of central importance to people's lives, it remains only a distant second. People do not become human beings through their work – and also are not justified through work. People receive their identity as God's gift and grace and can only then find meaning and fulfillment in their work«.[37] This is an example of taking seriously the »distinction

35 MERCEDES LAUENSTEIN, Gelassenheit. Die Generation Y setzt sich mit ihrem Wunsch nach einem erfüllten Arbeitsleben selbst unnötig unter Druck, in: jetzt (magazine of Süddeutsche Zeitung), Nr. 1/2017, 16.

36 KATHARINA DÖBLER, Die Tyrannei des Glücklichseins. Wie der herrschende Glücksbegriff uns das Leben schwer macht, Deutschlandradio Kultur, 9.11.2014, online: http://www.deutschlandradiokultur.de/kommentar-die-tyrannei-des-gluecklichseins.2162.de.html?dram:article_id=302665 (accessed: 8.5.2017).

37 COUNCIL OF THE EVANGELICAL CHURCH IN GERMANY/RAT DER EKD (Ed.), Solidarität und Selbstbestimmung im Wandel der Arbeitswelt. Eine Denkschrift, Gütersloh 2015, 63.

between our Selves and our Actions«[38] established by the Reformation, while at the same time acknowledging that they are reciprocally related.

Work is indeed a significant point of intersection between human selfhood, a gift from God, and human action (or at least it can be). That is why the expectations of meaningfulness as described above are definitely on the right track, even if it would be a mistake to turn them into an absolute. They take seriously the fact that work is not only (and not necessarily) something external. It has something to do with the God-given selfhood of human beings and is a key medium through which we can be active in the world. Not without reason did Luther speak of Man as »Cooperator dei« (»cooperator of God«).[39] The »Ethnographer of Cancer Care«, the »Treehouse Builder« and the political scientist »who's Passionate About Progress«: all these »vocations« we met at the start represent not only the yearning for meaning but also the passion for worldly activity whether on a smaller or a larger scale.

It is the aim of the contributions to this volume to demonstrate that the concept of vocation introduced by the Reformation provides us with a way of thinking about human labour that remains relevant to contemporary life; and that this is because it places as much emphasis on the dignity and the social dimension of work as on the importance of a correctly-understood passivity.[40] At the same time, this collection shows that this understanding of vocation also implies specific demands on the living reality of work, to make it appropriate – that is, respectful of human

38 DIETRICH KORSCH, Antwort auf Grundfragen christlichen Glaubens. Dogmatik als integrative Disziplin, Tübingen 2016, 172.

39 Cf. BERNHARD LOHSE, Luthers Theologie, Göttingen 1995, 259.

40 The Memorandum of the Council of the Evangelical Church in Germany evokes Eberhard Jüngel's concept of »creative passivity«, a willingness to allow oneself to receive gifts and talents from God (COUNCIL OF THE EVANGELICAL CHURCH IN GERMANY: Solidarität [see note 37], 63).

Annalena

qualified architect, on maternity leave at
the time of the interview

»Every day, my work represents a new challenge for me. Although the same activities always recur, each time it involves something new, and each time something unexpected as well. For me, being a mother is not a job, but rather a feeling or an instinct. Compared with my job, I can't learn how to be a mother by studying or on a course, but through living day-to-day with my child. But I do believe that being a mother can be a vocation.

I became an architect because I find the professional field very interesting – the combination of technology and creativity. I find the interaction between these two fields exciting and challenging.

I get particular pleasure from the completion of a project, that is, when the building is finished. So, really, it is the beginning and end of a project that are the best bits. The beginning because you're taking on a new task, you start creatively from a blank sheet, nothing is fixed and you can think freely. The end because you see what has become of the first ideas and all that you have achieved.

Sometimes I find the stressful stages of construction management a bit of a problem, because you always have to be available for people to talk to, sometimes you're getting calls at half past six in the morning because there's always rain getting in somewhere again.

If money didn't come into it, yes, I would still like to continue in architecture, but perhaps more of the building-schools-in-Africa kind, or something else community-oriented, something that would enable me to use my skills. For example, designing or building accommodation for refugees.

My wish for my future career is to have exciting projects, nice developers, and less pressure with regard to time and costs in those projects. I would also wish to be better paid. And right now, a better way of balancing my life with my work.«

dignity.[41] This applies particularly to the jobs and advancement opportunities available to the unemployed and those with lower formal qualifications.[42] The Swedish theologian Gustaf Wingren emphasised as long ago as 1980 that the Reformation concept of vocation applies not only to the »higher professions« but to *all* vocations and occupations. This concept of vocation thus represents a legacy that carries with it responsibilities. It is possible that the ongoing and increasing digitalisation of the world of work[43] means that the true test of the viability of this concept still lies ahead.

41   Cf. TORSTEN MEIREIS, Arbeit als Beruf – eine protestantische Perspektive, in: HEINRICH BEDFORD-STROHM et al. (Ed.s), Arbeitswelten (=Jahrbuch Sozialer Protestantismus, Bd. 5), Gütersloh 2011, 38–41.

42   On the perspective of the unemployed, see the contribution by ANTJE BEDNAREK-GILLAND, Sinn und Sinnlosigkeit im Leben von Langzeitarbeitslosen, in: ANIKA FÜSER/GUNTHER SCHENDEL/JÜRGEN SCHÖNWITZ (Ed.s): Wie aktuell ist das reformatorische Berufsverständnis? For the Social Sciences Institute (SI) of the Evangelical Church in Germany (EKD), Leipzig 2017.

43   Cf. ERIC BRYNJOLFSSON/ANDREW MCAFEE, The Second Machine Age, New York 2016; RYAN EVENT, The Wealth of Humans: Work, Power, and Status in the Twenty-First Century, New York 2016; EUROPEAN POLITICAL STRATEGY CENTRE,The Future of Work. Skills and Resilience for a World of Change, Issue 13, 10 June 2016, online: http://ec.europa.eu/epsc/publications/strategic-notes/future-work_en (accessed: 8.5.2017).

*»In truth, there is nothing finer than self-exploitation –
that is, the use of one's own powers
for self-selected purposes,
if necessary to the point of exhaustion.
For that is human action, that is freedom.«*

(Ralf Dahrendorf, 1982)

Vocation – History and presence of a revolution

Gerhard Wegner

1. Introduction: Vocation – quite simply a revolution

It is beyond question that the ›discovery‹ of the idea of vocation during the Wittenberg Reformation by Martin Luther was one of the really significant innovations in religious and social history. Even a very contemporary study on *Employability* and the occupational system[1] cannot get by without referring to Luther. The fact that it was no longer only the rulers and the clergy who had a vocation or calling – i.e. a »given position« in society, deriving from God – but everyone: this was more than just a reform, it was quite simply a revolution.

»We should pursue our occupations with a happy conscience, and we should know that more is achieved through such work

---

1   Cf. KATRIN KRAUS, Vom Beruf zur Employability? Zur Theorie einer Pädagogik des Erwerbs, Wiesbaden 2006.

than if someone had founded all the monasteries and joined all the religious orders – be it the humblest housework.«[2]

The higher value accorded to the church and monastic callings (priest, monk, nun, bishop) is thereby destroyed. It is not possible for a righteous Christian to continue in such callings, where one lives contrary to the gospel, and to freedom, love and reason.[3] From that point on, the *vita contemplativa* ceases to be a luxury. »Once work is set apart as a distinct role, that is, as an occupation [...] then it becomes a real opportunity for everyone«.[4]

Since then, the principle that people have a calling has been one of the foundations of a fair society:

»Every man should lead a life such that he knows it pleases God, even if it is despised and lowly. To be a servant, a maid, a father, or a mother, are ways of life which are established and blessed through the divine word and which please God.«[5]

The social order and the religious calling from God come together in a manifest way in work which is brought into focus as the ›sense-form occupation‹.

What was behind this was a radical religious valorisation of ordinary, everyday life in one's occupation, marriage and family, which – to use modern terminology – accompanies raised self-awareness. This life now could and should be led according to God's plan, or to his greater glory.[6] Work becomes – spiritually,

---

2   MARTIN LUTHER, Sermon on Matth. 9,1ff., 5.10.1529, WA 29, 566, 39–567,20.

3   Cf. MARTIN LUTHER, De votis monasticis Martini Lutheri iudicium, 1521, WA 8, 573–669.

4   RALF DAHRENDORF, Wenn der Arbeitsgesellschaft die Arbeit ausgeht, in: JOACHIM MATTHES (Ed.): Krise der Arbeitsgesellschaft. Verhandlungen des 21. Deutschen Soziologentages in Bamberg 1982, Frankfurt a. M./New York 1983 32.

5   MARTIN LUTHER, Lectures on Isaiah 1527/29 / In Esaiam Scholia, 1532/34, WA 25, 385, 26–29.

6   Cf. CHARLES TAYLOR, Sources of the Self. The Making of the Modern Identity, Cambrigde ⁸2006, 221.

too – a very serious business. »From a Lutheran perspective, a person who does physical, secular work is in direct contact with God above. She or he needs no intermediary to achieve salvation«.[7] It follows that human beings are, by virtue of their calling, at one and the same time fully in the world and fully out of the world. They are fully active in this world and at the same time fully distanced from the world, and with God. It is the *use* of things that expresses this position.[8] The problem is no longer their utility as such but the intention behind their utilization. The consequence of this can be hesitancy: »We must enjoy things while remaining detached from them.«[9] »We must in one sense love the world, while in another sense detesting it.«[10] Carefulness and carefreeness at the same time.

»Use things, ›as if you used them not‹ [...]. Marriage and a calling are not optional extras; they are the substance of life, and we should throw ourselves into them purposefully. But all the while our hearts should be elsewhere.«[11]

It is this thoroughly paradoxical, not to say dizzying existential claim that maintains the Protestant work ethic. It can take different, even opposing directions: in an artistic, autopoetic self-stylisation as the consummation of my calling, with the attendant danger of autism; and at the same time in a totally drained, repetitive stream of activities which ends in annihilation through work. In each case, the required identification with work – for one's neighbour – always stands in relation to its potential emasculation and equalization. Our works have nothing to do with

---

7   Gustav Wingren, Luthers Lehre vom Beruf, München 1952 (FGLP 10/3), 664.

8   Cf. Taylor (see note 6), 221f.

9   Ibid., 222.

10   Ibid., 222.

11   Ibid., 223.

Christine

chemist, works as assistant study director
in an analytical laboratory

»My work is a very important part of my life, because you have to work to earn your living. But because you spend a very big part of your life there, for me it needs to be something I enjoy. The fact that I studied chemistry was a decision made on instinct. At school, chemistry was the thing I enjoyed most – I was good at it, and it came easy to me. At some point I discovered chemical analysis, and especially environmental chemical analysis. I enjoy it, I can do it, and for me it seems much more useful than organic or inorganic chemistry, the classical main areas.

What I particularly enjoy at work is when I find a mistake and I can then correct it. Sometimes that happens quickly, and sometimes it takes longer, but at some point it goes ›ping!‹ in your head and then you know what's going on. And then I enjoy preparing it again and telling the lab assistant how to test it. And when it works then, it just makes you very happy.

What I don't enjoy is when I don't have enough to do. If I'm twiddling my thumbs, then the time passes at a snail's pace. I much prefer it when I go home I know what I'm going to be doing the next day. Not when I have to look for something to do or to ask people to give me a task.

If money didn't come into it, I might perhaps have landed in the same job anyway, because I just studied what I was good at and what I enjoyed. I really didn't choose this line of work because of the money.

What I hope for in my future career is to become study director rather than assistant, because I can then work more independently. And also that I continue to enjoy it.«

justification. They happen only because they are needed by our neighbours. I do not need them myself. Work therefore certainly has a purpose, because it enables us to pursue aims – but it has no inherent meaning. In this sense I can and should work in my occupation – but I myself remain extrinsic to my work. It enables me to be a full member of society – but I stand entirely outside it and confronting it.

2. Work and career as bringing God into the world

From the very beginning in 1517 it was clear that »Beruf«, or »calling«, applied not only to gainful employment but in a very wide sense to social life in its entirety. A calling designates a specific position in society, which is linked to tasks, rights and obligations, and to which the individual person brings their given characteristics and capabilities and develops them for the good of all. A calling is therefore much more than just an activity that is beneficial in and to the world and that could be measured in terms of functionality and paid with money. It represents – in the sense of a vocation – a service to God.

»If every person were to serve their neighbour, then the whole world would be full of service to God. The servant in the stable and the boy at school serve God. If the maid and the mistress are pious, that is a service to God. In this way all houses would be full of service to God and our houses would become proud churches, because God would be served there.«[12]

This affirmation serves to endow work with great intrinsic value, indeed to make it an end in itself. Understood as a calling it becomes justified in itself – or perhaps in God – and does not rely on justification through what it achieves or through profit. In

---

12 MARTIN LUTHEr, Sermon on Matth. 22, 34ff., 29.9.1532, WA 36, 340, 12–16.

this sense, to have a calling – even after the religious rationale no longer applies – means far more than simply carrying out some kind of work. Seen as a calling, work is ennobled, and the human capacity to work is given especial recognition. For that reason, too, a calling means much more than is encompassed in the modern concept of (gainful) employment: to be called to work in the service of one's neighbour is something much greater than any form of gainful employment, and the concept of »calling« in this usage is derived from a broader understanding of God's call to us to practise worldly charity.

The logic runs as follows: I have been given to myself as a gift so that I can give myself to others. A calling actually originates in this specific exchange of gifts. It is precisely my vocation, and it is to be put into action through my occupations. My ›gifts‹, in the widest sense, are to be put to use in cooperative work in society. This vocation is reflected in personal attitudes: in values, virtues, in ideas of honour and shame – and also in institutions which symbolise those attitudes. »Calling« implies hard work and diligence on one's own initiative,[13] to which one is committed because it is justified in itself. In secular terms: the unique, personal inner core of one's being actively unfolds, and we come to see ourselves through this process. »Through the same process by means of which we realise our selves, we learn for the first time what this self is that we are realising.«[14]

The modern world of work certainly cannot be imagined without the aid of such ideas, but – and this is what is fascinating about it – it cannot really be imagined with them, either: to require too much of them by way of meaning inevitably leads us away from those enterprises that today shape the world of work. But not only

---

13   Cf. VOLKER GERHARDT, Selbstbestimmung. Das Prinzip Individualität, Stuttgart 1999, 28.

14   HANS JOAS, Die Kreativität des Handelns, Frankfurt a. M. 1996, 122.

that: this constellation of ideas – in secularised form – works in socio-political terms too. So in today's terms, someone is considered poor if they are not able to develop fully in line with their individual capabilities and character. This means that it is not only access to work or income that separates the poor from the not-poor, but precisely what is meant by a calling. And this is exactly what Luther meant. In spiritual terms, this means that poverty or wealth are decided by the possibility of realising one's vocation. What that might mean today has yet to be revealed. A ›calling to poverty‹, or the occupation of being poor, is no longer possible since the Reformation.

3. Taking people out of the world

However, it is also important to see that in Luther's thinking the realisation of one's vocation in one's occupation has very little to do with ›self-realisation‹ in the modern sense. It was about the realisation of a call ›from the outside‹, from God, in my service to others. A Christian lives not for himself, but for his neighbour – as Luther doesn't tire of repeating. Accordingly, it is the idea of duty which applies here, later to be so important an element of the Prussian-German virtues. To put it pointedly: I work not for myself, not to assert my self, but rather to do what is useful and necessary for others, for my neighbour. It follows that my calling or occupation includes the sense of carrying out an ›office‹ as a trustee or guardian. This can be raised to the point of selflessness, to a point where one has to suffer harm and injustice. The exercise of revenge or of rights is legitimate only when undertaken for others.

This principle of ›selfless responsibility‹ is possible because Luther was able to distinguish between the ›external‹ calling within the secular order and the spiritual, ›internal‹ vocation in the kingdom of God. Spiritually, the Christian man or woman lives fully by participating in God's reality – he or she has everything they need. And from a spiritual perspective all people are equal. But for precisely that reason, nobody should really fight for their own interests: the public space is ruled by passivity and contentment with one's lot. One should only strike when the authorities allow it.[15]

To put it another way: the religious world, which is characterised by the inclusion of the individual in a larger, overarching context of meaning, stands ›against‹ the world of everyday reproduction by providing experiences of completeness, of being in safe hands, and of an overwhelming benefaction of meaning. Whereas our everyday cares lead us to apply our strength in all kinds of activities in order to overcome the perpetually self-regenerating fundamental fear, the religious perspective articulates the experience of wholeness of, and sanctuary for, the self in an (in God's) all-encompassing reality. In the final analysis, the everyday world provides mechanical answers to fear and concern and in this way repeatedly undermines the possibility of real freedom for human beings. But a fundamentally religious temperament provides a framework for everyday life – and so for work in particular – which means that it is seen as meaningful and valuable in itself. It gives the individual a role in the whole of creation and a place in a greater, all-encompassing reality. Care is not banished from the world, but it can be shorn of its existential terror.

The motivation for work would then no longer be fear, but could be love. »Work is love made visible.«[16] Employment contracts can therefore always be understood also as »partial gift

---

15 Cf. WINGREN (see note 7), 664.

16 GERHARD WEGNER, »Work is love made visible« Theologische Anmerkungen zur grassierenden Arbeitslust, in: Jahrbuch Sozialer Protestantismus 5, 2011, pp. 248–253.

exchanges«,[17] which can always contain more than an exchange of work for money, but also »help«.[18] Luther takes this so far as to declare that the imitation of the saints is diabolic. To try to live like a saint is to abandon – precisely by trying to emulate a model – concrete love for one's neighbour. My actions then follow out of a desire to please God – and for that very reason they involve abandoning my neighbour.[19] There is no meaningful religious endeavour beyond my responsibilities in this world.

4. Calling and social status

Now, Luther's understanding of a calling has been much criticised in modern times. With this concept, it is said, Luther basically did nothing more than to reproduce in a new terminology the classical medieval social hierarchy embodied in the estates. According to Luther, one was called into an estate for life, and could not leave it. Thus his understanding of a calling offered huge support for social inequality at that time, even if it has to be conceded that the specific understanding of a calling or estate has nothing to do with despotic authority, with mutual exploitation or with the legitimation of hierarchic structures per se, but rather with the exercise of universal care and with love for one's fellows. In this sense Luther's concept of the estates was ultimately concerned with a functional order for society and not primarily with a ruling structure. However, for a modern, free society, this kind of thinking might no longer have any significance.

---

17 GEORGE A. AKERLOF, Labor Contracts as Partial Gift Exchange, in: The Quarterly Journal of Economics, Vol. XCVII, Nov. 1982 No. 4, pp. 543–568.

18 Cf. GÜNTHER ORTMANN, Als ob. Fiktionen und Organisationen, Wiesbaden 2004, 177.

19 Cf. WINGREN (see note 7), 662.

A similar interpretation of vocation – one with hard consequences – was propounded by the Hanoverian Lutheran and abbot of Loccum, Gerhard Uhlhorn, in his article of 1890, »The earthly calling of the Christian«. Uhlhorn emphasises that there is a heavenly vocation, in the sense meant by Luther, and thus that there is a heavenly and an earthly calling, but that they are not separate. It is wrong, he says, »to believe that one can only follow the heavenly calling by renouncing the earthly; rather, they are interwoven«;[20] and even more clearly: »by fulfilling one's earthly calling one also fulfils the heavenly one«.[21] In this context, there follows a discussion of material success as a criterion for the choice of a career. He argues that it is not a sin to strive »to further oneself through one's career, to become wealthier, or in other respects to work one's way upwards. But it is unchristian to practise one's occupation only in the pursuit of that goal«.[22] What is decisive is this.

»But whoever lives his earthly calling for the heavenly knows that he never works in vain. And however small and few his achievements: he achieves one thing, and that is the highest, and that is to make something of himself under the guidance of his God, for the kingdom of God.«[23]

Yet the inference drawn from this, which is elaborated at great length, cannot fail to be disconcerting to modern readers. It is that, for the sake of this testimonial and of the link to one's heavenly calling, one must never abandon one's chosen career. And this applies also to a career that has failed.

---

20 GERHARD UHLHORN, Schriften zur Sozialethik und Diakonie. Edited by MARTIN CORDES/HANS OTTE, Hannover 1990, 138.

21 Ibid., 138.

22 Ibid., 142.

23 Ibid., 142.

Gisela

social worker for people with special needs and coach for
social care, works as head of department in a facility for
people with disabilities

»My work is an important area of my life. Alongside my family, which is in first place, work is a big factor in terms of both time and content. I enjoy devoting myself to it, and I can develop and pursue my aims.

When I was about thirteen years old, my parents looked after a neighbour's boy who had a disability. It turned out that I was the one who could get on best with him. And besides that, it gave me real pleasure to do something together with him. And so I just continued with that, and did training courses that helped to firm up my career choice, and now I have been doing it for thirty years and I still enjoy it.

I get particular pleasure from spontaneous conversations with the residents, who enrich my life with their happy, friendly and open ways. So does working together with my colleagues. When we find solutions to the problems that need to be overcome, then I can go home satisfied.

What I find stressful are sickness epidemics, when lots of residents and at the same time lots of my colleagues are sick – that's a real challenge.

If money were not an issue, I would still do the same job. For me, choice of career is not dependent on money anyway. It's only right and proper that you're able to make a living from it – no question about that. But working with people, that's still what I would do – absolutely definitely!

For my future career, my hope is that I will be able to maintain the cheerful way I have of setting about problems or moving things forward. And that I can stay healthy – I won't be able to work if I don't.«

»To do what one can, with joyfulness and trust in God; to do so there, too, in bearing all of the heavy burden that a failed career brings with it, to prove oneself a Christian, in the confidence that those who love God must always and everywhere serve as best they can.«[24]

The underlying spirit of the conceptual framework of the medieval estates can still be perceived here, even if the terminology is different.

Now, it is interesting that Werner Elert, certainly no progressive thinker, should contradict Uhlhorn in his interpretation of Luther. The concept of a calling, he argues, is by no means a mirror image of the concept of the estates. This is because Luther carried the idea of individual vocation through into that of the calling. Belonging to a calling, in the sense of an estate, by no means guaranteed that one's daily work was also genuinely in the service of God. What was decisive according to Luther was that the motivation to work came from the vocation, and thus from God's will. »A Christian should do nothing that does not follow a divine command. This command is given through his calling. It is a gift from God that he sends us our fellow man, locates us amongst our neighbours and gives us our place in the governing system and in the family.«[25] This idea, he argues, creates a certain distance between vocation and occupation, and leads people to question continually whether they can really practice their vocation in their occupation. It is this which not only avoids raising barriers between people in the form of status groups or classes but actually removes them.[26] The search for work that suits my

---

24 Ibid., 139.

25 WERNER ELERT, Morphologie des Luthertums. Two volumes, München 1958 (originally 1931). Here vol. 2: Soziallehren und Sozialwirkungen des Luthertums, 67.

26 Cf. ibid, 67.

vocation, and for the right way to fulfil it, subjectivises and individualises the differing worlds of work and dissolves any class- or estate-based thinking. At the same time, it binds everyone to their fellows. »Love perpetually re-invents and re-shapes human activity within the framework created by the relationship to one's fellows.«[27]

Moreover, every genuine calling, because it derives from a ›divine vocation‹, demands the full engagement of the whole person. »No ethical value is to be accorded to achievement at work in itself, without taking account of how deeply someone has committed themselves to it.«[28] According to Elert, Luther criticised in this respect many aspects of the principle of a social order based on inherited status, and breached that principle. This was particularly true of his demand for access to education for all, including and especially girls and women. And he called for state scholarships for the children of poor parents. But this would only make sense if such an education might later open a path into a different social class from that of the parents. In that sense, Luther certainly did not permanently condemn anyone to the social class they were born into.[29] However, this was to change later, in a way that casts a darker light on Luther's concerns:

»The citizen of Luther's day is *also* a subject – but in his calling as in his house he has areas where according to the particular rules of conduct of his class and family he is free to do as he wishes. But the citizen of the Enlightenment era is *only* a subject.«[30]

It was not until the period of reforms at the beginning of the 19th century that the independent dignity of the citizen was restored, albeit with some limitations still. The same thing, he

---

27 WINGREN (see note 7), 665.

28 ELERT (see note 25), 68

29 Ibid., 73.

30 Ibid., 69.

maintains, applies to the crafts and skilled trades, where a great deal of Luther's understanding of a calling has persisted until today.[31]

5. Self-expectations and socialisation

Now, it will of course be necessary to subject to a critical debate this attempt to dig Luther's innovation out from under subsequent accretions. The question of the extent to which Luther believed people to be free from determination by their class remains open. But it is beyond question that Luther's basic approach of highlighting the individual's work as a calling in a social context against the background of the vocation of the self by God had a huge and pervasive impact over the following period. Ultimately, the seed sown by these statements grew and blossomed in the late 19th and 20th centuries, and led to forms of working life in which ever greater importance was placed on the aspiration towards self-realisation.[32] But this movement began much earlier: in essence, it has persisted since the Reformation, even if it has repeatedly been suppressed by measures adopted by those in power. If I am able to conceive of myself as having received my gifts and capabilities as a present from God, and thus as having a calling, then my actions are endowed with absolutely explosive and exclusive expectations from myself which have the potential to bring social barriers crashing down.

At the same time, my expectations suggest a tension which in Luther's thinking has already been worked through: between these expectations of and from myself and my reliance on those others among and for whom I am to practise my calling. This

---

31 Cf. ibid., 77.

32 Cf. e.g. KRAUS (see note 1), 143ff.

tension comes especially close to breaking point when probing questions are put about the process of vocation. In the Biblical tradition, of course, only a few people are actually directly called by God himself to serve him. As a rule, it is other people who in practice not only influence but actually articulate the vocation. »It is usually the parents and educators who are the mouth of God expressing the vocation.«[33] According to Luther they have a responsibility to take people's predispositions and preferences into account, but also to introduce each following generation to the vocations. Because this is so, a career is not the private concern of a single individual. »The reciprocal service carried out for each other, equally willingly, by two individuals, is always also in the service of the whole, whether they know and desire that or not.«[34] And this idea leads once again, very clearly, to the need for social subordination. In a modernised version, the discourse would be of cooperative occupational practice and of a cooperative realisation of occupational skills. Quite soon, we have arrived at modern vocational training, in effect a secularisation of this entire process. By the turn from the 19th to the 20th century, this has reached a point where a calling is determined more or less for life by the education system, »which is able to make use of the excess of meaning left available in the term by the decline of the religious component«.[35] This process reaches its conclusion in the Vocational Training Act of 1969.

Luther's thoughts on occupations and vocation were innovative and influential, but the upward revaluation of work in itself was already a general trait in Christian faith before Luther. The apostle Paul was proud of earning his living through the work of his own hands, and idleness was widely looked down upon. There

---

33 ELERT (see note 25), 74.

34 Ibid., 75.

35 KRAUS (see note 1), 149.

was a general tendency in the Christian world to make people »economic subjects«, as Michael Kittner summarises.[36] This implies an empowerment of the individual:

»The direct consequence of the body of Christian thought for the particular case of paid employment is easy to recognise. If the capacity for work is an expression of the personality of each individual, all equal before God, then the choice of how to apply that capacity for work is a free decision for which each is accountable. It follows inevitably that it is everyone's own choice whether or not to work for someone else.«[37]

And it is then this dynamic which leads to the development of the modern economic system, with all its contradictions and ambivalences, and of modern society into a kind of occupational utopia – one which no less a figure than Georg Simmel has succinctly and accurately characterised in his sociology. He analyses society procedurally as a process of socialisation in which people, as he puts it, must realise their specific characteristics, and their inner selves, to and for their lives as a whole. Only then can a society really function. Here, what is meant by a calling can already be heard in the background. But then it is stated more clearly:

»This behaviour acquires a certain intensification in the category of the occupation. The ancient world, it is true, did not recognise this concept in the sense of personal differentiation and of a society structured by working time. But what underlies it – the fact that socially effective action is the homogenous expression of internal qualification, that what is whole and persistent in subjectivity effectively objectivises itself by virtue of its function in society – that existed already in the ancient world.«[38]

---

36 Cf. MICHAEL KITTNER, Arbeitskampf. Geschichte – Recht – Gegenwart, München 2005, 37.

37 Ibid., 38.

38 GEORG SIMMEL, Soziologie. Untersuchungen über die Formen der Vergesellschaftung, Gesamtausgabe/Collected Works, Vol. 11, Frankfurt a. M. 1992, 60.

What is therefore expressed in this idea is »that the individuality of the person finds a place in the structure of the community, indeed, that that structure is to some extent designed in advance, in spite of the unpredictability of the individual, on the assumption of that individuality and its productiveness«.[39]

In contrast with experiences of total anonymity, a career is based on an inner calling:

»On a qualification which is perceived as entirely personal. In order for there to be a career at all, that harmony – whatever its origins – between the construction and living process of society on the one hand and the individual's nature and impulses on the other must be present. Because it is on this that the idea is ultimately based that for every personality there is a place and a role within society, one to which they are ›called‹, and the imperative to search for it as long as it takes to find it.«[40]

It is subjectivity seeking socialisation which finds itself in a career, and which is still present today in the idea of a career for which one is properly qualified. Accordingly, a just society is one in which people can pursue a career, i.e. their vocation or destined role.

6. Vocation as a critical category

And even if it is true that in the course of the formation of modern society the concept of a calling has increasingly been stripped of its explicitly religious character, yet it is always being made topical again in this sense, even in the 20th century. Thus, the Archbishop of Canterbury, William Temple, in an outstanding text in the context of the debate in Great Britain (»Christianity and Social

---

39   Ibid., 61.
40   Ibid., 60.

Hannah

trained to be a teacher of German and Music
and is a class teacher for pupils in Year 3

»I find my work very fulfilling, in the sense that it occupies me but also my life completely, sometimes very stressfully and often very joyfully – overall it is exactly the right work for me.

I became a primary school teacher because I wanted to work with children and to do something with music. This offered me the opportunity to combine both.

I really enjoy spending the day with children, who just have so many ideas and who give so much back. Whether it's just with words, when they say they think you're great, or when they hug you. Or just when they've understood something and they do things that they really shouldn't be able to do yet. I help them by giving them the freedom they need, by supporting them and helping them find their interests and their strengths.

There are always pupils who don't have it easy in their lives, and their stories weigh on me. And then there are always difficulties or disagreements among the staff, too, and with parents, and of course there are children who are difficult in class. And in addition, you don't get much chance to switch off, because there's no clocking-off time. You're always thinking about the children.

If money were irrelevant, I would do the same thing. I simply cannot imagine sitting at a desk the whole day, or carrying out a trade of some kind. Working with children – that's what I like to do.

My wish is for the school system to be revolutionised in several respects. So that children enjoy learning. Then I can be the kind of teacher I want to be. I can advise and support and offer help, but I don't have to drum stuff into them. Luckily, at the school where I teach, things are moving further and further in that direction.«

Order«), emphasises – just as Uhlhorn does – that it is possible to take on bad work if this is expected of one in a particular calling or, to put it another way, if it seems to be a duty. He goes on to say:

»Of course, this does not justify an order of society which offers to many men only such forms of livelihood as require a miracle of grace to appear as forms of true vocation. But we must recognise that the source of my vocation is in God and not in me. It is His call to me. And when it is said that we need to create or restore a sense of vocation in relation to all the activities of men, it does not mean chiefly that every individual should be able to find there his self-expression or self-fulfilment otherwise than by self-sacrifice. But it does mean, first that he should do his work, interesting or dreary, »as unto the Lord«, and secondly that the alternatives presented be such as shall not make this insuperably difficult apart from a true miracle of grace.«[41]

A calling is realised in »Freedom, Fellowship and Service«; which ultimately means that »the aim of a Christian social order is the fullest possible development of individual personality in the widest and deepest possible fellowship«.[42]

With these maxims at the back of their minds, many Christian writers on social ethics were critical of forms of work in which it is no longer possible to experience something like a professional career or a genuine calling. Thus William Temple required that »every citizen should have a voice in the conduct of a business or industry which is carried on by means of his labour, and the satisfaction of knowing that his labour is directed to the well-being of the community«.[43] From this point it is not a big step to a fundamental criticism of capitalism.

---

41 WILLIAM TEMPLE, Christianity and Social Order. London 1976 (first published 1942), 75.

42 Ibid., 97.

43 Ibid., 97.

»To many it appears evident that we have allowed the making of profits [...] to get into the first place which properly belongs to the supply of human needs [...]. We have inverted the ›natural order‹. Instead of finance existing to facilitate production and production existing to supply needs, the supply of needs is made the means to profitable production; and production itself is controlled as much as it is facilitated by finance.«[44]

Similar views can also be found in texts in social ethics at the end of the 20th century. In the rationale of this argumentation, unemployment and poverty are understood to be a waste of God's gifts. For example, in an outstanding position statement from the Anglican Church in 1997 on the issue of unemployment (»Unemployment and the future of work«), the following can be read. »Society as a whole suffers if the gifts of God are wasted, because they are meant to complement one another. No one can achieve their full potential unless we all do so together [...]. No one should be left out of the common task. No one should be told that their contribution is not wanted.«[45] And: »the whole idea of a vocation or calling will seem quite unrealistic to many people who are now unemployed. That is another reason why unemployment is so abhorrent to the Christian understanding of work and society«.[46] Elsewhere, good work for all is called for. »A better way of putting it would be to say that we all have a calling to serve one another and no one should be denied the opportunity to carry it out.«[47] A calling, in this perspective, is not only a spiritual event affecting a person's inner being, but can explicitly be experienced externally, for example in the very fact of access to employment – and then, too, in whether it is possible to carry out

---

44   Ibid., 96.
45   ANGLICAN CHURCH, Unemployment and the Future of Work, London 1997, 71f.
46   Ibid., 162.
47   Ibid., 81.

good work there. If someone has no access to these opportunities and is therefore prevented from being able to engage their own capabilities, he or she is poor in both a religious and a social sense.

7. Capabilities

These considerations recur, almost entirely unaltered in terms of content, in highly modern and prominently visible analytic discussions of empowerment and participatory equality, for example in articles published by the EKD and above all in the texts of Amartya Sen and Martha C. Nussbaum. In the case of these two authors the religious rationale has long been abandoned or forgotten, but the core of what the Reformation brought into the world clearly remains as an implied foundation. All these concepts start from the assumption that people possess inherent basic capabilities which need to be, as it were, drawn upwards and outwards through the processes of education and training so that people are able to realise their capabilities in cooperation in society. This is what constitutes human dignity. »The notion of dignity is closely related to the idea of active striving. It is thus a close relative of the notion of basic capability, something inherent in the person that exerts a claim that it should be developed.«[48] Human dignity requires that all people are treated equally not only in the sense that their capabilities are given the opportunity to develop, but also, and for the same reason, that they are treated differently, precisely because their capabilities are different.

»If people are considered as citizens, the claims of all citizens are equal. Equality holds a primitive place in the theory at this point, although its role will be confirmed by its fit with the rest

---

48 Martha Nussbaum, Creating Capabilities. The human development approach, Cambridge 2011, 31.

of the theory. From the assumption of equal dignity, it does not follow that all the centrally important capabilities are to be equalized. Treating people as equals may not entail equalizing the living conditions of all.«[49]

The approach from the perspective of capabilities therefore implies – as does the approach from the perspective of vocation – not that all people are materially equal, but rather the opposite: that they are in fact unequal, and that the development of their capabilities must be carried out in a way that enables them to complement each other cooperatively in society.

8. Commodification of work

It is only too clear that Luther's original provocations have not resulted in anything like a programmatic adoption of his ideas after 1517; this is perhaps even less the case in the later developments in the 17th and 18th centuries during the time of highly authoritarian state power. The great crisis in the thinking around vocation and occupation did not set in at this time, however, but at the beginning of the 19th century, with the rise of industrialisation and the modern capitalist economy. This was the start of something Luther had in some respects foreseen and warned against, namely the subordination of the calling as an end in itself to its external criteria of success and profitability. Work was taken out of its relational context (thus also out of the estates and guilds) and brutally exposed to the developing markets. Christians, too, supported this process, in the hope that it would lead to the conquest of poverty. A prominent example is the text »A Dissertation on the Poor Laws« (1786) by Joseph Townsend, which pleads for a radical marketization of the labour force. »Hope and fear are the

---

49 Ibid., 31.

springs of industry. It is the part of a good politician to strengthen these: but our laws weaken the one and destroy the other.«[50]

Karl Polanyi described this process in England very clearly in his book »The Great Transformation«;[51] similar analyses can be found much earlier, for example in the work of Karl Marx. The formulations in the Communist Manifesto are classic examples.

»In proportion as the bourgeoisie, i.e., capital, is developed, in the same proportion is the proletariat, the modern working class, developed – a class of labourers, who live only so long as they find work, and who find work only so long as their labour increases capital. These labourers, who must sell themselves piecemeal, are a commodity, like every other article of commerce, and are consequently exposed to all the vicissitudes of competition, to all the fluctuations of the market. Owing to the extensive use of machinery, and to the division of labour, the work of the proletarians has lost all individual character, and, consequently, all charm for the workman. He becomes an appendage of the machine, and it is only the most simple, most monotonous, and most easily acquired knack, that is required of him.«[52]

However, Utopia lays claim to the old ideals:

»In place of the old bourgeois society, with its classes and class antagonisms, we shall have an association, in which the free development of each is the condition for the free development of all.«[53]

What was to be realised, in religious terms, in one's calling – the free development of the self in the interests of others – is now

---

50   Cf. http:// socserv.mcmaster.ca/~econ/ugcm/3ll3/townsend/poorlaw.html (accessed: 8.5.2017).

51   KARL POLANYI, The Great Transformation. The Political and Economic Origins of our Time (first published 1944), Boston 2001.

52   Cf. https://www.marxists.org/archive/marx/works/download/pdf/Manifesto.pdf (accessed: 8.5.2017).

53   Ibid.

secularised as the goal of a communist society. The aim is the »interweaving of the productive activity of all to form a community that produces and enjoys the fruits itself«.[54] »Each of us in our production would have *in two ways affirmed* himself and the other person.«[55]

The nature of work had changed in such a way that the concepts of vocation and calling were no longer plausible.

»To separate labor from other activities of life and to subject it to the laws of the market was to annihilate all organic forms of existence and to replace them by a different type of organization, an atomistic and individualistic one.«[56]

All previously existing forms of communal security and thus also of the valuation of work are destroyed by the expansion of the markets with their anonymous pressures.

»The creation of goods involved neither the reciprocating attitudes of mutual aid; nor the concern of the householder for those whose needs are left to his care; nor the craftsman's pride in the exercise of his trade; nor the satisfaction of public praise – nothing but the plain motive of gain so familiar to the man whose profession is buying and selling.«[57]

Human society, Polanyi concluded, had become no more than an »accessory of the economic system«.[58]

A disgust at this loss of occupational structure and of individuality and identity can be clearly perceived in the debates among conservative Christians. They recognise that this represents a turn away from older ideas and social structures but are for the

---

54 JOAS (see note 14), 138.

55 KARL MARX, Auszüge aus James Mills Buch, in: MEW, Ergänzungsband/Supplement 1, Berlin 1968, 462.

56 POLANYI (see note 51), 171.

57 Ibid., 77.

58 Ibid, 79.

most part unable to grasp the structural causes, let alone to do away with them through reforms.

Consequently, there began a dispute which has continued to the present day over the reclamation of employment as an autonomously meaningful understanding of vocation. Polanyi reported that in England, at least, the industrial working class continued for a long time to ask if salvation lay »in a return to a rural existence and to the conditions of handicraft«.[59] But such hopes remained illusory in the face of the economic superiority of the new economic structures. The old bands of class had to be broken – liberation from pre-capitalist restraints was necessary to enable accumulation and thus a revolution in productivity.

»Only within a generalized system of commodity production and exchange, including the purchase and sale of the capacity to labour itself (›labour-power‹) was it possible for the ›economic‹ to become seperated from the other spheres of life.«[60] And this is what sets off the revolution of needs. Only when exchange value holds sway are all the borders set up ›naturally‹ by use value broken down.

In that sense, everything connected with the ideal of a calling could only be reclaimed over the longer term once the new dynamic had established itself, and certainly not in opposition to it. The struggles around this transition were long and complex. Many diverse interests were involved. Central among them were, on the one side, capital interests, which instrumentalise and revolutionise perceptions of employment structures, and on the other side the direct interests of the workers, who fall back on some aspects of structured employment in their own interest, to enable them to defend their autonomy and maintain their capacity to

---

59 Ibid., 175.

60 GARETH STEDMAN JONES, Introduction, in: Karl Marx und Friedrich Engels: The Communist Manifesto. With an introduction by G. St. Jones, London 2002, 181.

work. Polanyi demonstrates impressively how this conflict led to the development of the labour movement in the 19th century, and how great was the role played in this by traditional religious justifications of the value of work. What was still inherent in the idea of a calling, namely the emphasis on the value of the individual person and on making it ultimately a criterion for work, fades ever further from view for the mass of the population in the face of industrialisation and capitalisation.

9. The crisis of vocational work and its rediscovery

This development reaches its zenith in the 20th century with the emergence of purely mechanical forms of work such as in the Tayloristor and Fordist systems. Here, the workers have finally been reduced – with the aid of science and technology – to appendages of the machines, and their work, viewed from the outside, appears to have no meaning in itself, since it has been reduced to purely mechanical motions. »No factory worker can interpret his own mechanised labour as his ›calling‹ any longer«.[61] Consequently, movements arose in opposition to this, which were accompanied in Germany in the 70s and 80s by projects for the humanisation of work, and thus also led to a rediscovery of the value of vocational work. »The Protestant work ethic can only interpret in the light of the Christian faith work which is within a career structure and which still involves an elemental measure of interpersonal relationships and individual discretion and responsibility«.[62] This development constrained the ability of the churches even to understand factory workers, let alone to ›help‹ them in any way.

---

61 WINGREN (see note 7), 667.

62 Ibid., 667.

Johannes

lawyer, works as compliance officer and in-house
lawyer for an insurance company

»My work is an important part of my life. I can commit myself to what I do and identify with it. I find my work exciting and interesting and I have a great many really nice work colleagues, so I really enjoy going to work.

When I began studying law, I didn't have any firm ideas about my future career, I just wanted to find out more about the legal system and everything connected with it and to understand it.

I particularly enjoy it when I am giving advice or teaching on a course and I can see that I have been able to help people and that they have learnt something. I enjoy the atmosphere at work with my colleagues. Lunchtimes we go to get something to eat, and people tell each other what they're doing and often it's great fun.

What I don't enjoy at work is when it gets stressful. When we've got a lot to do and I can tell that we are letting people down because they have to wait for an answer from us, for example, and we can't respond in good time because we have ten other things that have to be done first. That is unsatisfactory. But up until now I have never felt that I was unable to leave it behind me when it was time to go home.

If money was irrelevant, I would definitely like to devote more time to music, but I don't know if I would give up my job completely. Perhaps just reduce my working hours a bit and then see how it goes.

My hope for my future career is that I can continue to work with such nice colleagues. And that I can continue in my present role – I can certainly carry on doing that for a long time if the team stays as it is. That really would be the most important thing.«

From a Protestant perspective, the critical observation has to be made that in the mutilation of humanity carried out in the name of Taylorism and Fordism can be found one part of the historical legacy of Protestant work-based asceticism. The religious wellsprings of an ascetic self-sacrifice on the altar of Work, the renunciation of any form of diversion from the utmost concentration of the faculties – adopted at some point from monastic meditation techniques and strictures – are reflected in secular form in the sacrifice of people to the machine. If originally there was still a religious structuring rationale to this, now that rationale can be found only in a different external instance – in increasing consumption. Work itself becomes meaningless, and this is intentional. Moreover, the view of human nature associated with Taylorism, which views people as essentially lazy and only susceptible to extrinsic motivation, found many points of reference in Protestant thinking. In any event, Protestantism certainly played its part, for good and ill, in the epochal task of making mankind fit for modern work.

It was not humanitarian considerations that brought this form of production to crisis point, but the fact that it reached its productive limits. This was closely connected with the transition from mass production to more difficult and sophisticated, more individualistic and customised forms. In such forms, quality could no longer be assured by excluding the subjectivity or the individual intelligence of the workers, but only through better use of such factors. At the end of the 1980s and the beginning of the 1990s, this led to downright revolutionary changes at the workplace: for example, the introduction of autonomous and quasi-autonomous group work in the car industry,[63] where much

---

63 Cf. Eva SENGHAAS-KNOBLOCH/BRIGITTE NAGLER/ANNETTE DOHMS, Zukunft der industriellen Arbeitskultur. Persönliche Sinnansprüche und Gruppenarbeit, Münster 1996.

more trust than before was placed in the capacity of the workers for self-organisation, and the human factor was to that degree able to have more impact. Substantial increases in productivity were achieved in this way. This all exemplifies »how far autonomy can be forcibly introduced into heteronomy«.[64]

These developments received further impetus from the adoption, from the 1990s onwards, of ever more varieties of project work, involving flexible working time (e.g. trust-based working time), management by objectives, etc. Today such forms are typical of the world of work in many sectors, especially among higher qualified workers. This oft-cited ›organisational revolution‹ at work has been greeted euphorically as a liberation of individual intelligence and of intrinsic motivation. The reduced emphasis on units of activity which are clearly defined and therefore susceptible to monitoring, and which tended to constrain the potential productiveness of work, in favour of broader conceptions of work and of (self-)realising activities on the part of the workers, was – for a time at least – visible everywhere, and a surprise to many observers. It was possible to come across observations like the following. »An exciting process [...] is taking place in the factories: the liberation of the workers' intelligence [...]. We are experiencing the revolt of the person against control from without. This parallels the Renaissance, which ultimately led to the Reformation. The contemporary second Renaissance seems to be connected with a climate of reform.«[65] A re-birth of all that had been associated with vocational work and careers seemed to be in the offing.

In this, firms were reacting to the changing wishes of employees, who were no longer prepared to submit to dehumanised and fragmented working conditions. In general, it can be observed

---

64 DAHRENDORF (see note 4), 35.

65 GERHARD SCHMIDTCHEN, Lebenssinn und Arbeitswelt. Orientierungen in Unternehmen, Gütersloh 1996, 31, 33.

that the classic phenomenon of alienation in the workplace, still widely diagnosed during the 60s and 70s in connection with Taylorist and Fordist worksystems, has in many sectors retreated into the background over the last thirty years. It also became noticeably more troublesome – because it provoked more conflict – to practise long-term, detailed monitoring of productivity. So it made sense to expose the workers directly, to a far greater degree than before, to market conditions, i.e. to the wishes of clients, and to entrust them with the fulfilment of those wishes (with all the consequences). Concepts such as ›flat hierarchy‹ (lean production, lean management) were part of an attempt to increase the subjective identification of workers with their work by giving them a higher measure of decision-making responsibility. At times this even led to discussions about the abolition of the management level, or of bosses in general. However, with the end of the 90s and the beginning of the 21st century, this movement, too, came up against specific productivity limits, and it was possible to observe a re-introduction of some forms of Taylorist work processes, albeit with higher levels of self-management.

But Schmidtchen's observation of 1996 is correct:

»The Prussian-puritan model of behaviour control was a failure to the degree that employees were dependent on communication to complete their tasks accurately and without errors, and needed to apply their experience and intelligence independently at work and not just to carry out orders. It became more and more apparent that employees who were only required to follow instructions in carrying out repetitive tasks were unable to use their intelligence.«[66]

And furthermore: »Passivity and distrust are barriers to the flow of information at the workplace. It transpires that appropriate organisational structures which encourage an active style of

---

66 Ibid., 38.

task completion raise self-esteem and recognition at the workplace; in short, they generate stability of purpose.«[67] And it is clear that all this serves to confirm structured working careers as the principal source of intrinsic work motivation. In contrast, where the work capacity of the employees is regarded purely as a substitutable resource, machines are cheaper in the final analysis.

The highly ambivalent situation apparent here is shaping the world of work today. Workers are being given much more freedom and room to organise themselves than used to be the case. The strengthening of ›bottom-up‹ as opposed to ›top-down‹ relations, the promotion of networks leading to the development of heterarchies rather than hierarchies, the huge importance of communicative negotiation processes as opposed to directives – all of this strengthens the spread of freedom and autonomy and enables work to be experienced as something positive and not alienated.

Nevertheless, the situation remains asymmetrical. The independence and autonomy of the employees have now become resources for management. Their exploitation enables product quality to be improved and volatility in production processes to be avoided. Something which came into play as a form of resistance has now been co-opted. »You can do anything you like as long as it's profitable!« is the credo. The recognition of one's own dependence is reshaped as acceptance. What was seen as compulsion must now be presented as compliance. From more freedom comes more pressure. And this is the undoing of significant numbers of workers.

What has now entered the stage is the idea of a »new occupationalism«.[68] It is distinctive in its allocation of identi-

---

67 Ibid., 75.

68 Cf. KRAUS (see note 1).

fication and distance, and in that it deviates from old Lutheran distinctions – without however even knowing them. The new occupationalism is characterised by, among other things, a low level of institutionalisation, qualifications which tend towards the abstract, high levels of flexibility, individualisation and self-organising skills, a tendency towards decontextualisation of vocational/occupational learning processes and low demarcation barriers.[69] Translated into religious terms: there is a simultaneous increase in people's detachment from the world – they conceive of themselves ever more firmly as separate and abstracted from the concrete living reality of work – and in their attachment to it, their determined and efficient grasp of the concrete situation.

10. I am a gift

But that is not all there is to say about the fate of the relationship between vocation and occupation in modern times. As can be seen already in the almost prophetic observations of Georg Simmel, the modern era has seen the evolution of a form of individualism centred on the self in response to the collapse of classical forms of community and their associated natural processes of socialisation. People in the modern era are obliged to emphasise authenticity and personal experience in the creation of their own biography, and to be constantly developing their own normativity. The longer this process goes on, the more they fight for the recognition of hitherto deviant behaviour as socially acceptable. The logical implication of the principle of inclusion is the full recognition of precisely that which – or those who – may be alien in an unwelcome way. They, too, have been gifted with themselves.

---

69 Cf. RITA MEYER, Der Beruf als »Sinnform« von Arbeit, in: Loccumer Protokolle 66/02, Loccum 2002, 82.

»The liberation of the individual, occasioned by socio-struc-
tural forces, increasingly confronts people against this background
with the challenge of acquiring certainties for the structuring of
their lives which they need in order to remain capable of changing
direction in a world which is too complex to understand.«[70]

To put it more pointedly: modern human beings are required
to construct their own identities and to continually re-invent
them. So society's complexity, vulnerability and diversity are
internalised in the individual, and this leads to a perpetual growth
and development of people's inner lives, an evolution of the self,
which then turns outwards in many respects in its demand for
gratification. The world of occupational employment responds to
these energies and at the same time exploits them. Social impera-
tives, too, such as independence, participation and creativity, and
ultimately also that of individual entrepreneurial activity, drive
economic development forward.

»Whereas before behaviour was predominantly steered by
external impulses (models), today the importance of self-disci-
pline is growing. An ability to handle responsibly the options that
present themselves and the freedom for manoeuvre must be developed in parallel with this, and directed towards a morally-based
self-governance.«[71]

In this context, the question of how to measure inner progress
in a social environment fraught with risk presents itself in a new
and decisive way.[72] If one translates this situation into the classical terminology, then it appears that today more than ever peo-

70 Hans-Joachim Höhn, Soziologie in der Theologie – oder: Der Blick von
    außen auf den Blick nach außen, in: Ansgar Kreutzer/Franz Gruber
    (Ed.s): Im Dialog. Systematische Theologie und Religionssoziologie, QD,
    vol. 258, Freiburg i. Br./Basel/Wien 2013, 70.

71 Jürgen Weibler, Werthaltungen junger Führungskräfte (Böckler Forschungs-
    monitoring, vol. 4), Düsseldorf 2008, 37.

72 Cf. ibid.

Lea Sophia

is training to be a physiotherapist

»For me, my work is my vocation. It's my view that everybody is guided to do the thing they do best. I believe my work is the meaning in my life.

I would like to become a physiotherapist because it's work that never becomes boring. I'm always on the go, and that's good for me and for my body. And I can help lots of people and change their lives by doing so.

I particularly enjoy my job when what I do is successful. When I can see that what I'm doing with a patient is finally taking effect. But even just when a patient smiles when I come in, and we understand each other well – those are happy moments.

What I find difficult is when patients could do more themselves but just don't bother. We are supposed to bring the best out of our patients if at all possible, but when you keep having to motivate them further and it has no effect, that's hard.

If money was irrelevant, I would start my own practice. There would be a wellness area with a big swimming pool with an adjustable-depth floor. Then you really can get any patient in. But in any event, I would want to continue as a physiotherapist. Because I'm doing well myself, I want things to go well for others too.

What I wish for my further career – because of course money does come into it – is that we in the social sector in general could get a bit more money. If only just for all the training courses we have to do. But also so that more people feel they can take the risk of going to work in the social sector. I think it just puts people off to have to pay for their training, given that it's so difficult anyway and that later on you hardly earn anything from it. You even have to save up a bit longer than most people if you want to go on holiday once in a while.«

ple have to be clear about their own »vocation« – that is, about who they really are and what they really want. And it is easy to predict that in this respect it is possible for pathologies of pure self-absorption to arise which could be pre-empted or counteracted through a qualified conception of vocation as a triangular relationship between me, the other and God. It seems that people's religious sense of self has retreated, so to speak, into a form of inner monologue; but this means that it has most certainly not disappeared. The fundamental idea, however, that I am gifted with myself, and that I have the duty and the right to work through this narrow self-absorbed perspective and to bring it to bear in social cooperation, remains not only important but is potentially highly beneficial for the shaping of work and society.

The tension described here presents itself as a gulf between the liberation of a surfeit of opportunities for self-realization at work and a reduction in their number by means of recurrent organisational revisions. Thus we experience today ever more hitherto unknown forms of delight and inspiration at and through work – but also related and frustrating experiences of disillusionment and disappointment resulting from our own occupational engagement and commitment. The interaction of productive capacities and energies at individual and organisational levels always leads at one and the same time to forms of identification and increased productivity as well as to new forms of disappointment, distress and strain. Work-related pathologies have recently increased across a broad range, and it is increasingly open to question whether these can be put down to problems of transition and/or familiarisation. So a public debate is called for about the downside to the growth in freedom at the workplace – that is, about new forms of self-exploitation, about psychological dependency on work, about burnout symptoms and the growth in mental illness.

11. The future of jobs

People are more self-confident today than they used to be in their dealings with firms, and that is a good thing. They seek personal gains in terms of self-affirmation, competence, good relations and fun at work.[73]

»What is sought is a dynamic relationship between the individual and the firm. The individual thinks and judges for him- or herself and intervenes in the life of the firm to give direction and to improve. In this way employees can satisfy their own self-image, develop their personality through the working life of the firm, gain respect and acquire stability for other life contexts.«[74]

This would represent the return of the calling. However, this development also carries serious risks, since it can involve the loss of the healthy distance from one's own actions that was an essential component of the original religious concept. Work can then – as absurd as this may sound – become a pleasure in itself, and become addictive in some way. That in turn means withdrawal treatment. We should not place undue expectations on work to provide us with meaning in life.

Therefore: the call should not be, »Be who you are!«, but rather, »Become who you should be!« A calling in this sense feeds on the relationship to my self coming from God, which is both alien and personal at the same time. It is not only the perpetual question to myself that drives me[75] but the questioning of myself, which sets free a self-confident, active individual as a freely and knowingly accepted dependant. »For it is precisely this *capacity for self-limitation*, the possibility of *freely deciding to be or do something*

---

73   Cf. SCHMIDTCHEN (see note 65), 43.

74   Ibid., 46.

75   Cf. GERHARDT (see note 13), 30.

in the full consciousness of one's own limitations, which engenders the illimitable dignity and worth of a human being«.[76]

And it was precisely this that was the starting point for Luther's deliberations. Falk Wagner ends his great study of vocation as follows:

»Under the contemporary conditions of advanced industrial society, it is only rarely possible to ascribe the practice of an occupation in the pursuit of gainful employment to a specific vocation. Nevertheless, it is not impossible to set the occupational activity in the context of the fulfilment of a freedom initiated by a vocation. The occupational activity will then be practised within socio-economic structures which enable working people to make use of their acknowledged freedom.«[77]

If it is true that behind the idea of a vocation there stood at one time the reassuring – but also deeply constricting – idea of a cosmos in which every creature has its allotted place, such that »self-knowledge would consist of discovering and taking up this place«,[78] then today that idea is reversed and has become an imperative – namely that of overthrowing all those relationships which served as obstacles to the full development and realisation of human communicative capabilities.

76 Ibid., 138.

77 Falk Wagner, Berufung III. Dogmatisch, in: TRE, Vol. 5, Berlin/New York 1980, 713.

78 Joas (see note 14), 121.

»God at Work« or, What Workplace Spirituality has to say about vocation

Gunther Schendel

1. »A call to a spiritual purpose« – the new discourse of vocation

»How can I integrate the values of my faith into my workaday life?« This question about the relationship between faith-based convictions and everyday life was posed by the head of a major New York asset management company[1], and it is typical of a trend in the USA calling for the workplace to become somewhere where employers and employees do not hide their faith or spirituality but bring it with them. This trend exists in Germany, too, where a few years ago a newspaper report on the Congress of Christian business leaders and on regular »bankers' prayer meetings« in Frankfurt was headlined »God is a growing new presence in working life in Germany«.[2] But it is considerably stronger in the USA, and researchers and others involved in the field of management and consultancy there have given it its own label: »Workplace Spirituality«.[3]

This movement is of interest to us because the issue of *vocation* or *calling* plays a central role in it. A US academic who works

---

1   PETER C. HILL/GARY S. SMITH, Coming to terms with spirituality and religion in the workplace, in: ROBERT A. GIACALONE/CAROLE L. JURKIEWICZ, (Ed.s): Handbook of Workplace Spirituality and Organisational Performance, London ²2015, 171–184, 180.

2   AXEL GLOGER, Gott hält vermehrt Einzug ins deutsche Arbeitsleben, in: WELT, 27.12.2010, online: https://www.welt.de/wirtschaft/karriere/leadership/article11803438/Gott-haelt-vermehrt-Einzug-ins-deutsche-Arbeitsleben.html (accessed: 8.2.2017).

3   Cf. e.g. GIACALONE/JURKIEWICZ, Handbook (see note 1).

on the connection between environmental awareness and corporate culture writes that »many employees are finding a *call* to a spiritual purpose by bringing social values, such as environmental protection, into the workplace in order to serve the greater good of society. And many employers are recognizing this shift and attempting to channel this energy towards the mutual gain of employer and employee«.[4] And two other US researchers working on the connection between management and spirituality identify a specific category of employees who understand their work as a form of ministry, as a service and a means of serving others. According to the researchers, they do so out of the conviction that »God placed them in their workplace and position for a greater purpose«.[5]

These two quotations from the literature on *Workplace Spirituality* demonstrate already that »vocation« can imply very different levels of specificity and of religious content. Sometimes it can signify a specific value such as environmental protection, at other times it can signify the religious conviction that one has been placed somewhere by God. The issue of vocation comes up time and again in the extensive literature on *Workplace Spirituality*. Some authors mention it only briefly, though its significance is taken as read; others set out a detailed conceptual schema of vocation, one that – sometimes consciously – diverges from fixed religious interpretation and dogma.

In this article, these new concepts of vocation will be outlined and subjected to analysis. In addition to the inherent value pro-

---

4 Andrew J. Hoffman, Reconciling Professional and Personal Value Systems. The Spiritually Motivated Manager as Organizational Entrepeneur, in: Giacalone/Jurkiewicz, Handbook (see note 1), 155–170, 155 (emphasis added).

5 David W. Miller/Timothy Ewest, The Integration Box (TIB): An Individual and Institutional Faith, Religion, and Spirituality at Work Assessment Tool, in: Judi Neal (Ed.), The Handbook of Faith and Spirituality in the Workplace. Emerging Trends and Research, New York 2013, 403–416, 410.

vided by such an analysis, we hope to throw light on the question of whether these interpretations of vocation can help in our search for a re-formulation of the Reformation idea of vocation and calling that is relevant to the modern world and theologically sound.

2. Workplace Spirituality – a brief overview of the movement and the concepts involved

Before we turn to the analysis of these concepts of vocation, an outline of the broad field of *Workplace Spirituality* (WPS) may be useful for orientation. Nowadays there are manuals and periodicals devoted to this topic, as well as research and further education institutes; there is a course on »Spirituality and Business Leadership«[6], and several metrics for »Faith and Spirituality at Work«[7]; and there are even prizes for »Spirit at Work«.[8] In addition, the US Academy of Management has a Section devoted to »Management, Spirituality and Religion«.[9] WPS thus shows several faces to the world simultaneously: it can be encountered as a new »paradigm« in management and other areas of research[10]; it is a scientific concept; and it describes the programme of a specific approach to management. But at the same time, WPS shows some characteristics of a cultural »movement«[11] in which people with a shared mindset join forces to create a structured common body.

6   NEAL, Handbook (see note 5), 14ff.

7   Ibid., 383.

8   Ibid., 16.

9   AOM/Academy of Management: Management Spirituality and Religion, 2016, online: http://aom.org/Divisions-and-Interest-Groups/Management-Spirituality-and-Religion/Management-Spirituality-and-Religion.aspx.

10 GIACALONE/JURKIEWICZ, Handbook (see note 1), 10.

11 NEAL, Handbook (see note 5), 4.

2.1 A new paradigm

This new paradigm emerged in the early 1990s[12], and can be described as an extension of an older management theory, as exemplified in Elton Mayo's Human Relations movement.[13] Mayo, of course, focused on employees as social beings rather than (as Taylorism had done) simply as appendages of the production machinery. WPS now brought into focus the spiritual dimension of the employees' lives, their »spiritual energy« and their values.[14] Today such »soft elements« are a familiar feature of the corporate marketing of large firms[15], for example in their projection of fundamental ethical values and social and ecological responsibility within the framework of *Corporate Social Responsibility* (CSR).[16] WPS is thus a part of a broader development in which – for example, through the introduction of flatter corporate hierarchies – employees are given more autonomy, or companies project themselves as »good employers« in order to gain the cooperation, motivation and loyalty of their employees. Empirical evidence for the positive effects of integrating »spirituality«[17] and values into corporate culture has been provided by numerous international studies since the 1980s. Spirituality at the level of the individual, and an organi-

---

12 GIACALONE/JURKIEWICZ, Handbook (see note 1), 3.

13 NEAL, Handbook (see note 5), 5.

14 NEAL, Handbook (see note 5), 5.

15 For the situation in Germany cf. KLAUS KAIRIES/ERNST SCHROTT, Zur Relevanz der Entwicklung von Spiritualität für die Realisierung von »Corporate Social Responsibility (CSR)«, Arbeitspapier Hannover 2008, online: https:// serwiss.bib.hs-hannover.de/files/307/CSR_Arbeitsbericht_2008.pdf (accessed: 8.2.2017).

16 SCHNEIDER, Spiritualität und Spirituality in der Welt der Arbeit und der Welt der Gesundheit, International Journal of Practical Theology, 2012, Vol. 16/1, 152.

17 In the WPS literature, for example, this is defined as »optimism, an orientation toward giving, acceptance of diversity« (GIACALONE/JURKIEWICZ, Handbook [see note 1], 9).

sational culture which is open to spirituality, have been shown to contribute to contentment at work[18]; furthermore, it is correlated with finding a »sense of purpose«, with a reduction in absenteeism and with higher productivity.[19] Such »Workplace benefits«[20] have contributed to making WPS a new topic of organisational culture for management.[21]

2.2 Value shifts and »Workplace benefits«

At the same time, the growing interest in WPS can be understood as the result of a shift in values towards a post-materialist outlook, as described by Ronald Inglehart as early as the 1970s.[22] His work documents a growing number of people in the USA with a post-materialist orientation. A core group among them is that of the »Cultural Creatives«, who are interested in self-realization, have a spiritual outlook, and are socially engaged and ecologically aware.[23] The idea that one's values should not simply be put to one side at the entrance to the workplace[24], an idea often cited in the

---

18 Ibid., 9.

19 TIM HAGEMANN, Arbeit, Gesundheit, Spiritualität & Religiosität. Forschun gsbericht, Fachhochschule der Diakonie 2012, 3, online: https://www.si-ekd.de/download/Hagemann_Vortag_Pflege.pdf (accessed: 8.2.2017).

20 SCHNEIDER, Spiritualität (see note 16), 147.

21 For Germany, cf. the debate on spiritual resources in the caring professions and diaconal identity, cf. DIAKONISCHES WERK DER EKD/JOHANNES STOCK-MEIER/ASTRID GIEBEL/HEIKE LUBATSCH, Geistesgegenwärtig pflegen. Existenzielle Kommunikation und spirituelle Ressourcen im Pflegeberuf, 2 Bde., Neukirchen-Vluyn 2012/213; HEIKE LUBATSCH, Führung macht den Unterschied – Arbeitsbedingungen diakonischer Pflege im Krankenhaus, Münster 2012 (= SI konkret 5).

22 GIACALONE/JURKIEWICZ, Handbook (see note 1), 14.

23 Ibid., 15.

24 KELLY PHIPPS/MARGARET BENEFIEL, Spirituality and Religion. Seeking a Juxtaposition that Supports Research in the Field of Faith and Spirituality at Work, in: NEAL, Handbook (see note 5), 33–46, 34.

Michael

self-employed master
carpenter and designer

»For me, my work is a part of my life. It gives me pleasure to create things and to leave behind something that will last.

Ever since I learned to think, I have put things together – little ships, oak guns, swords and so on – in my father's workshop; he was a carpenter himself. I was always working with wood. And as the son of a craftsman I was in touch with the business side of it from the beginning. I don't think I would be so ful-filled, so busy or so content in any other walk of life.

What I enjoy most is when I go to see people who want something altered, and then afterwards it's just as they had imagined. What I find interesting about my job is that as time goes on you learn so much more, and that it's really only as a self-employed person that you have the chance to work in all aspects of the job, not just fitting windows or dry construction.

What I find stressful as a one-man company is when I miscal-culate the time required for a job, or when I fall ill, and as a result a backlog of work builds up. Also, you need to beware that you don't overestimate your abilities. That you only do what you're sure you can do. If you try to do too many differ-ent things by yourself, that can be difficult sometimes. And if it's something new, then you just have to seek advice and make sure that it's done properly.

If money didn't come into it, I would build dream houses, from start to finish. Finding plots of land, designing houses, and building them and selling them to people who appreciate what you've done for them. I would want to create something I could be proud of. Something that would be so good, so beautiful or so out of the ordinary that others would want to have the same thing too.

My wish for my future career is that I will always have enough work and will stay healthy.«

WPS literature, applies particularly to this group.[25] Instead, they aim »to bring their whole self to work«.[26] It is post-materialist »Cultural Creatives« of this kind who are responsible for some of the writing on WPS: for example, Judi Neal, the editor of a voluminous »Handbook of Faith and Spirituality in the Workplace«, refers enthusiastically to Marilyn Ferguson's »Aquarian Conspiracy«, a key text for the New Age movement.[27] Neal's handbook contains contributions on the topic of »Faith at Work« from representatives not only of the three Abrahamic religions – Judaism, Christianity and Islam – but of Eastern and indigenous faiths and practices (for example Tibetan Buddhism, Yoga, Aborigines and Maori).

This underlines again the breadth of the WPS phenomenon, which in the USA lies behind a wide range of commercial services on offer. For example, there are several thousand »Corporate Chaplains«, who can be booked, through agencies, to provide »hope« and »caring« at the workplace[28]; there is a self-styled »Corporate Shaman«, ready to »heal and restore spirit to organizations«.[29] WPS thus presents a very diverse picture, and is by no means restricted to those of a post-materialist bent: the theologically conservative Southern Baptist Convention also pro-

---

25 According to a Gallup survey in the USA in the late 1990s, 48% of those surveyed had had an opportunity in the preceding 24 hours to speak about their religious faith at the workplace (see JUDI NEAL, Creating Enlightened Organizations: Four Gateways to Spirit at Work, New York 2013, 18).

26 DAVID W. MILLER/ TIMOTHY EWEST, Faith at Work. Religious Perspectives: Protestant Accents in Faith and Work, in: NEAL, Handbook (see note 5), 69–84, 76.

27 NEAL, Handbook (see note 5), 4.

28 Corporate Chaplains of America, 2016, online: http://chaplain.org/ (accessed: 8.2.2017).

29 The Corporate Shaman, 2017, online: http://corpshaman.com/ (accessed: 9.2.2017).

vides Corporate Chaplains[30], though there is a clear gap between their set of values and post-materialism.[31]

The more we learn about this area, the more pressing becomes the question of what exactly WPS is. Is WPS a catch-all term, like spirituality[32], of which it is said that its great virtue lies in »not having to be exact«?[33] And indeed there is, within the field of WPS, a widespread »soft approach« involving discussion in the workplace of issues such as caring, empathy and mutual support, from an individual and personal perspective.[34] However, along-side this and in contrast to it, the academic literature offers pre-cisely formulated concepts and definitions as well.

2.3 Between a catch-all term and precise definitions

One substantive issue is the relationship between spirituality and religion. In the literature on WPS, a huge variety of defini-tions of this relationship can be found, ranging from those that define WPS without any reference to religion whatsoever to those that assume (whether consciously or not) an exact identification between the two. One way of distinguishing between them, pro-posed by Brian J. Zinnbauer among others, is by focusing on the level at which the discourse takes place. Spirituality is the appro-

---

30 North American Mission Board, Corporate Chaplaincy, 2016, online: https://www.namb.net/chaplaincy/corporate (accessed: 8.2.2017).

31 Cf. Detlef Pollack/Gergely Rosta, Religion in der Moderne. Ein interna-tionaler Vergleich, Frankfurt a. M. 2015, 381.

32 Thomas Klie according to Evelyn Finger, Die Renaissance der Unver-nunft: Sehnsucht nach dem Selbst, DIE ZEIT, 16. Mai 2013, http://www.zeit.de/2013/21/esoterik-vernunft-verteidigung/komplettansicht (accessed: 8.2.2017).

33 Michael Beintker, Christliche Spiritualität – Versuch einer Kriteriologie, in: Hans Krech/Udo Hahn (Ed.s), Lutherische Spiritualität – lebendiger Glaube im Alltag, Hannover 2005, 39–61, 39.

34 Giacalone/Jurkiewicz, Handbook (see note 1), 11f.

priate term, it is argued, when the subject at hand is the individual experience of transcendence at the micro level; whereas religion is taken to refer to the institutional or meso level, for example when the subject is theology or ritual.[35]

The desire to make a clear distinction between spirituality and religion derives not only from a thirst for scientific precision but also from the particular situation in the USA. On the one hand, interest in WPS is strong; on the other, in the context of the constitutional separation of church and state and of increasing confessional and ideological pluralism, there is a strong a priori wish to avoid a definition of spirituality that is closely tied – let alone exclusively tied – to a single religious faith: »Models of workplace spirituality aligned with particular religious expressions would rightly be rejected by industry«.[36] Moreover, a growing number of US citizens make a distinction in their own minds between religion and spirituality: nine percent describe themselves as »spiritual but not religious«.[37] Notwithstanding this, researchers such as Kelly Phipps and Margaret Benefiel advocate a model involving not only a distinction but also a transition zone

---

35 PHIPPS/BENEFIEL, Spirituality (see note 24), 34–36. Robert Wuthnow makes the distinction between »dwelling« and »seeking spirituality«, so differentiating between a security-resp. certainty-oriented attitude and one which is more experimental (according to HILL/SMITH, Spirituality [see note 1], 176ff.).

36 PHIPPS/BENEFIEL, Spirituality (see note 24), 37. In the influential »Academy of Management« literature »one sometimes senses a thinly veiled disdain for religion and a preference for spirituality, the former seen as restrictive and inappropriate and the latter seen as welcoming and more inclusive« (MILLER/EWEST, Faith (see note 26), 75). For the development of the relationship between religion or more precisely WPS and public service labour law in the USA cf. RICHARD D. WHITE, Drawing the Line: Religion and Spirituality in the Workplace, in: GIACALONE/ JURKIEWICZ, Handbook (see note 1), 185–196, 187ff.

37 POLLACK/ROSTA, Religion (see note 31), 355. Cf. MARK OPPENHEIMER, Examining the Growth of the »Spiritual but Not Religious«, New York Times 18.7.2014, online: https://www.nytimes.com/2014/07/19/us/examining-the-growth-of-the-spiritual-but-not-religious.html (accessed: 8.2.2017).

between spirituality and religion (»distinct but overlapping«[38]). They point to empirical evidence that deeply religious people do not feel the need to distinguish clearly between spirituality and religion, whereas the distinction is important for less religious people.[39]

An academic definition of WPS that can be very widely applied comes from Robert A. Giacalone and Carole L. Jurkiewicz: they define WPS as »aspects of the workplace, either in the individual, the group, or the organization, that promote individual feelings of satisfaction through transcendence«.[40] This is a definition that is open to interpretations of WPS based on content as well as function.[41] »Transcendence« is used to refer to what it is that the various strands of belief and research concerning spirituality at the workplace have in common. And the »promotion of feelings of satisfaction« in the workplace refers to the positive practical effects anticipated from this form of spirituality. Another advantage of this definition is that it is by no means limited to the individual, but also encompasses groups and organisations. This means it is applicable to the whole range of phenomena described above: WPS is of course not just a matter of individuals bringing their values and their own ideas associated with transcendence into the workplace, but a question of organisational culture, of teamwork and leadership.

This relativization of any purely individualist perspective is especially important when we widen our horizon to include non-Western societies. The South African theologian Thabo Mak-

---

38 PHIPPS/BENEFIEL, Spirituality (see note 24), 39.

39 Ibid., 36 and 39.

40 GIACALONE/JURKIEWICZ, Handbook (see note 1), 13.

41 Sociologists of religion make a similar distinction between an understanding of religion based on form and one based on function (GERT PICKEL, Religionssoziologie. Eine Einführung in zentrale Themenbereiche, Wiesbaden 2011, 21).

goba, for example, draws on the concept of Ubuntu, which emphasizes the interplay between individual and society, to construct a
critique of any form of WPS focused solely on the welfare of the
individual and on a purely internal transcendence.[42] In this way,
Makgoba goes beyond the definition cited above and formulates
on the basis of the concept of Ubuntu a normative »spirituality of
compassion and social justice« which expresses a transformative
interpretation of spirituality, one that is concerned to bring about
change at the workplace.[43] He rejects any instrumentalization of
WPS aimed at raising productivity or restricted to a palliative role
and concerned only with the inner life of the individual.[44] This
example shows that the WPS concept can certainly have relevance
outside Western society as well, and indeed that in a post-colonial
context it can be given sharper focus by the addition of a socio-
ethical dimension.

---

42 THABO MAKGOBA, Workplace Spirituality: In a South African Mining Context –
    A Reflection from a perspective of spinal cord injured mine workers, Saarbrücken
    2011, 220f.

43 THABO MAKGOBA/KURT APRIL/AKRAM AL ARISS, Understanding Spir-
    ituality at Work, Organizations and in Management, in: Academy of Taiwan
    Business Management Review, 2014, online: http://www.kurtapril.co.za/index.
    php?option=com_docman&task=doc_download&gid=100&Itemid= (accessed:
    8.2.2017), 41–52, 46.

44 MAKGOBA, Workplace Spirituality (see note 42), 231; MAKGOBA/APRIL/AL
    ARISS, Understanding Spirituality (see note 43), 48. In matters of spirituality,
    Makgoba and his co-authors identify three distinct trends: the »palliative«, the
    »via media« and the »transformative trend« (MAKGOBA/APRIL/AL ARISS,
    Understanding Spirituality [see note 43], 45f.). In the »palliative trend«, the indi-
    vidual perspective is foregrounded; alongside »interiority« the authors identify the
    capacity for compassion as a defining feature (45). They place the »transformative
    trend« at the other end of the scale, wherein individuals become prophetic »agents
    of change in the world« and the links between spirituality and specific religions are
    subjected to critical examination (46). The »via media trend« occupies the space
    in between, not confining spirituality to interiority but opening it up to concern
    for the community and for human rights and liberation theology (45). The »via
    media trend« is supported by influential authors from the USA and Great Britain
    such as Philipp Sheldrake and Rowan Williams. However, according to Magkoba
    and his co-authors, the »transformative trend« is especially compatible with »Af-
    rican spirituality« (45).

3. »Find your Calling«[45] – concepts of vocation in Workplace Spirituality

But let us now turn our attention to the differing interpretations of the concept of vocation found in the literature on WPS. The US sociologist Robert J. Wuthnow found in a survey of workers in the United States in 1993 that »they did not think of their work as a calling nor did they understand the concept of stewardship«.[46] As already noted, however, there is also a counter-movement against this form of secularization, a »resurgent interest« in the connections between work and spirituality or religion.[47] Concepts of vocation represent in this context a significant hinge or connecting link between the world of work and the transcendent, so it is worth taking a closer look at the various forms this connection takes.

In what follows, we will look at two very different conceptual categories with regard to vocation. First, we will examine two concepts with a clear orientation towards the Protestant tradition, and thus a decidedly religious basis. Then we will turn our attention to an eclectic-syncretic concept that is consciously »spiritual« in orientation.

3.1 Protestant concepts – beyond the classical work ethic?

The influential US literary scholar Leland Ryken described the classical Protestant concept of »vocation« or »calling« as a »cluster of related ideas«. In his view, this »cluster« includes belief in

---

45 Neal, Creating (see note 25), 24.

46 Hill/Smith, Spirituality (see note 1), 179.

47 Ibid. On the »processes of de-differentiation« identified by sociologists of religion in the USA, cf. Pollack/Rosta, Religion (see note 31), 378.

God's »providence [...] in arranging human work«; respect for work as providing an opportunity for the »response of a steward to God«; and »contentment in one's tasks«.[48]

This definition brings together a number of substantial points regarded (in the contemporary WPS literature as well) as defining features of the Protestant conception of vocation:

- a high regard for work (Hill and Smith, drawing on Luther and Calvin, go so far as to speak of a »sacralization of all occupations«)[49]
- a personal identification with work as a task given by God
- finally, a particular vocational ethic that seeks more than purely personal gain in any work (the fact that it was perfectly possible to combine this with striving for profit is demonstrated by historical examples from among the Moravians and the Quakers, who made the profits from their businesses available to the community or for missionary projects).[50]

In contemporary Protestant concepts, the idea of »vocation« or »calling« plays a role in two ways. Firstly, in the sense of *vocation as a given task*, meaning the fulfilment of the *purpose* of being a Christian in this world. Secondly, in the sense of *vocation as personal discovery*, that is, the question of how a Christian discovers her or his personal calling.

---

48 Leland Ryken, Redeeming the Time: A Christian Approach to Work and Leisure, Grand Rapids 1995, 106, from Hill/Smith, Spirituality (see note 1), 178.

49 Hill/Smith, Spirituality (see note 1), 178.

50 Cf. Miller/Ewest, Faith (see note 26), 74.

Vocation as task

What is the task to which Christians are called in this world? David W. Miller and Timothy Ewest, management scientists and theologians in the »Faith & Work Initiative« at Princeton University[51], summarise the task as follows: »Protestants believe that individual Christians are called to participate in God's creation, even in fallen state, through the already completed redemption in Jesus Christ, by cocreating and helping restore the fallen world and reform it afresh in God's image«.[52] Miller and Ewest are referring here to the idea of human beings as cocreators, which can be found today in Lutheran theology as well.[53] This cocreation goes beyond the conservation and preservation of the world and is conceived of as a concrete aid to the completion of God's work of salvation: »There is a sense of duty to complete God's creative work«, »a call to heal and repair the broken or fallen aspects of the material world«.[54]

The call thus leads Christians into a broad range of activities in the world. The fact that such an approach resonates beyond denominational borders is shown by the South African theologian and Methodist pastor Dion Forster, who speaks explicitly of a »social transformation« »for the good of humanity and the estab-

---

51 It was not possible to establish with certainty the denomination of the two authors. Ewest teaches at a Baptist university (Houston Baptist University 2016: personal web page for Timothy Ewest, online: https://www.hbu.edu/contact/timothy-ewest/, accessed: 8.2.2017).

52 MILLER/EWEST, Faith (see note 26), 82.

53 The US Lutheran Philipp J. Hefner calls human beings »created cocreators« (STEFAN SCHÜTZE, Heute glaubwürdig von Gott reden: »Gott«, »Mensch« und »Welt« im 21. Jahrhundert, Hamburg 2014, 35). Luther rejected talk of human beings as »cocreators« because he wished to emphasize human beings as part of Creation and preferred to speak of them as »co-workers« within it (BERNHARD LOHSE, Luthers Theologie, Göttingen 1995, 259). In that sense, Hefner is picking up and taking forward Luther's concern.

54 MILLER/EWEST, Faith (see note 26), 79.

Mirja

studied theology and is currently a vicar
(training to be a pastor)

»At the moment, my work is a big part of my life. It is something like a vocation because I can never completely switch it off. But that doesn't bother me.

I want to be a pastor because that is a career in which I can do what is really important to me and get paid for it: being a point of contact and help for people at the important moments in their lives. Of course, God plays a part in this as well. Faith is something very important to me, and I can tell people about it and help them to live out their own faith.

I really like to hold church services. But I enjoy just as much sitting all alone at home and occupying myself quietly with reading the Bible and preparing the service. But I really derive great joy from those moments when others are there as well, for example at ceremonies like baptisms or weddings. That gives me really great pleasure. I'm the one who prepares everything and holds it all together, and so I can say to the others, ›You can enjoy yourselves now and you don't have to worry because I will see to it that everything runs smoothly.‹

Bereavement conversations can be very stressful, if someone's story touches me because it triggers something personal in me. And at the moment I find still being constantly tested and evaluated stressful, too. You see then how dependent you are within the bigger system.

If money didn't play any part, I would still want to be a pastor. You don't do it to earn money.

I would like a congregation where I can be a good pastor, and I would like to master the challenge of balancing work with my private life.«

lishment of the Kingdom of God«.[55] Both of these representative concepts share a particular approach to eschatology. Whereas the Protestant work ethic, in Max Weber's classical description, was based on the assumption that the Kingdom of God was not of this world (leaving to one side for a moment the indirect confirmation by God of the status of the Elect by means of their success in the business world), Miller and Ewest identify »a move away from eschatological thought« in contemporary Protestantism.[56] They point to Reinhold Niebuhr's »Christian Realism«[57] as one source of their concept of active Protestant engagement in the world, while Forster cites the Third Lausanne Congress on World Evangelization[58] in support of his transformational approach, and he also interprets the concept of »Missio Dei« correspondingly.[59]

It is interesting then to see what specific forms of socio-ethical action Miller/Ewest and Forster go on to cite. How should the call to action in the world be put into concrete practice? Miller and Ewest identify several features of a contemporary Protestant work ethic. Alongside the practice of one's vocation in daily life and fulfilling one's role as »cocreator«, acting in accordance with »economic justice and business ethics« is important, as are a certain lifestyle and bearing witness to one's faith (»evangelism/ expression«), including in the workplace. As a good example of

55   DION FORSTER, Called to work: a descriptive analysis of Call 42's research on faith and work in South Africa, Koers – Bulletin for Christian Scholarship, vol. 79/2 (2014), 1–9, online: https://www.researchgate.net/ publication/273455780_2143-5901-5-PB_Koers_Final_Galleys_21_November_2014 (accessed: 8.2.2017), 7.

56   MILLER/EWEST, Faith (see note 26), 78.

57   Ibid.

58   FORSTER, Called (see note 55), 8. The Congress took place in Cape Town; the concluding document (The Cape Town Commitment: A Confession of Faith and a Call to Action, 2010) can be found at https://www.lausanne.org/content/ctc/ ctcommitment (accessed: 3.3.2017).

59   Ibid., 6. On the concept of Missio dei cf. ANDREAS GRÜNSCHLOSS, Missio Dei, in: RGG, Vol. 5, Tübingen ⁴2002, 1271–1272, 1271f.

how to interpret one's role as »cocreator« and of the Christian duty of »stewardship«, they cite Robert Greenleaf's management theory concept of »servant leadership«, which sees leadership as service and empowerment (»enabling them to do their jobs better«).[60] Miller and Ewest believe that economic justice entails acting responsibly at all levels: honesty and integrity are just as important here as an international economic system based on fairness and an awareness of the impact of one's economic actions on those less powerful. One's way of living should be characterised by a mixture of »lifestyle modesty« and a »spirit of radical generosity«[61]; and tithing is praised »as a minimum way of thanking God for His generosity and helping those less fortunate«.[62] Bearing witness to one's faith in the workplace can take verbal form, but it can also occur by example (»charity« and »willingness to suffer for the other«).[63]

Miller and Ewest thus offer a very wide-ranging concept of vocation in practice, one to which Forster adds a specific dimension drawn from his South African context, namely that of the fight against corruption.[64] It is clear, though, that both models of how the Protestant work ethic can be given contemporary relevance focus primarily on the working lives of managers and others in leadership roles.[65] The working experience of employees with less decision-making responsibility receives less attention.

---

60 MILLER/EWEST, Faith (see note 26), 79–81.

61 Ibid., 80.

62 Ibid., 81.

63 Ibid.

64 FORSTER, Called (see note 55), 7.

65 Forster also makes the same criticism of the current literature on WPS (FORSTER, Called [see note 55], 7).

Vocation as personal discovery

How and where do Christians find their vocation? This question has been addressed in the Protestant tradition via the concepts of »Vocatio specialis« and »Vocatio externa«.[66] In this field, there are two concepts in the contemporary WPS literature with a long ecclesiastical tradition: vocation as discontinuity/rupture, and vocation as finding a new direction in one's given station and location. The idea of vocation as a discontinuity or rupture is relatively rare, but can be found in the Pentecostal movement. For example, the establishment of a Christian publishing house still operating successfully today is traced back to an act of prayer by two pastors, who would regularly »pray about God's calling for them«, and who, having achieved clarity over their path, sold their houses and arranged to move to a different city.[67]

Forster doesn't entirely ignore the question of the proper location for the practice of one's vocation. He cites the exhortation of the evangelical Anglican theologian Miroslav Volf that some activities or jobs should not be carried out: sex work, drug dealing or taking part in crime are less »desirable« than care or taking part in the overcoming of structural oppression.[68] Here he is referring to moral norms and ethical values. More important for his argument, however, is the certainty that God has given everyone a »unique« and »divine design«[69], which is to be discovered through prayer and to be realized and lived in »radical

---

66 FALK WAGNER, Berufung III. Dogmatisch, TRE, Bd. 5, Tübingen 1980, 688–713, 691f.

67 LAURA ALLISON AKIN, A Business Case Study of DaySpring Cards, Inc., in: Neal, Handbook (see note 5), 535–564, 538.

68 FORSTER, Called (see note 55), 8.

69 Ibid., 28; 33.

obedience«.[70] Behind this lies a particular interpretation of God's »spiritual gifts«, which are to unfold fully in and to the glory of God and the service of one's neighbour; this is the only way for the human »longing for meaning«[71] to find fulfilment. Does this necessarily have to result in a radical departure from one's life up to that point? Not according to Forster: usually, the most important location for the deployment of one's spiritual gifts is the place where one lives (»[...] it is fairly likely that God will want to use you where you are«).[72] Another reason for this is that God does not want to cast aside valuable relationships and highly developed faculties, but to use them.[73]

Forster's conception of vocation is thus marked by continuity: it is not necessarily about a change of location, or a new job[74], but about a new attitude, one that gives expression to one's gifts and capabilities in the service of humanity and to the glory of God.[75] This understanding of vocation draws on certain elements of the Reformation tradition, such as the priority given to continuity, to service, and the focus on the glory of God (which plays an especially important role in the Reformed vocational ethic). However, here these elements are utilized for a missionary transformation of the world: in Forster's view, the gulf between faith and work, between Sundays and workdays, must be overcome because of the importance of »establishing God's kingdom in Your workplace«.[76]

---

70 Ibid., 36; 116.

71 ibid, 7.

72 GRAHAM POWER/DION FORSTER, Transform your Life. Turn an ordinary day into an extraordinary calling, Petaling Jaya 2010, 35.

73 Ibid.

74 Forster nevertheless does not exclude the possibility of changing jobs in order to live out one's »passion« (POWER/FORSTER, Transform [see note 72], 35).

75 FORSTER, Called (see note 55), 6.

76 POWER/FORSTER, Transform (see note 72), 69.

Interim conclusions

What is impressive about the concepts of vocation described above is their conspicuous commitment to the integration of faith and work. This is supported by the structural framework of a work ethic characterised by a powerful desire for practical engagement in the world – it is precisely for that reason that identifying and carrying out one's vocation has so much importance. The broad social agenda to which the individual's working life is supposed to contribute is impressive. It calls to mind the ethos of liberal social reform which Ernst Troeltsch one hundred years ago ascribed to the new Calvinist and Anglo-Saxon churches, and which he contrasted with the »interiority« of Lutheranism.[77] The fundamental asceticism that Troeltsch detected in the »New Calvinism« of his day can also be found again in the calls to »modesty«. However, this can nevertheless still be reconciled with a contemporary focus on postmaterialism.

What is ›modern‹ are the yearning for meaning, and the idea of the individual's talents as gifts of God's grace; here, a link is being made to how people experience their lives in the era of individualism. However, God – as Forster sees it – is here very much an external and distinct presence whose call and intention are clearly perceptible. This absence of ambiguity needs to be problematized, as does the focus of these concepts on the higher and middle management levels. How does vocation apply to people whose primary concern is with their material security, who do not have the resources that will liberate them for the pursuit of their

---

77 ERNST TROELTSCH, Die Soziallehren der christlichen Kirchen und Gruppen, Teilband II, Tübingen 1912 (= reprint Tübingen 1994), 790. The link between action in the world, a personal image of God and the »de-differentiation« of religion and other spheres of life in contemporary religiosity in the USA is pointed out by POLLACK/ROSTA, Religion (see note 31), 378f.

passions?[78] And how do fragmented, discontinuous working lives fit into this concept?[79]

3.2 Beyond traditional confessional conceptions of vocation – Judi Neal's fluid spiritual concept

Following this consideration of Protestant concepts of vocation, we now want to continue by considering an approach which does *not* analyse vocation against the background of a particular confessional tradition. Judi Neal, who has been cited here several times already, is a former consultant and university professor of management now working amongst other things as a coach.[80] She has developed a concept of »calling« that goes beyond its Protestant roots in order to place at its core »a much more universal longing for meaning and purpose in work«.[81] Although she draws on various religious traditions (Buddhism and Hinduism in addition to the three Abrahamic religions), she is principally concerned with »spirituality«, and specifically with the question of the meaning of human life.[82] Much like Forster, she believes that »[t]here is a growing consensus that each of us has a mission and purpose in this lifetime«[83] in which our respective gifts

---

78 POWER/FORSTER, Transform (see note 72), 35.

79 Graham Power and Dion Forster, under the heading »What if I am not the Boss?«, address only the example of a secretary who prays for her boss – material problems or precarious working conditions are not dealt with (op. cit., 157; 162).

80 JUDI NEAL, Bio, 2007, online: http://www.judineal.com/pages/corporate/nealbio. htm (accessed: 8.2.2017).

81 NEAL, Creating (see note 25), 23.

82 Op. cit., 32.

83 Ibid.

Ruth

a trained nurse, working as night supervisor in an old people's home and as an unpaid voluntary pregnancy counsellor

»For me, work is for the most part a source of joy. ›Fulfilment‹ is a very big word, but it goes in that direction. It makes me happy when other people are happy.

Already as a child I used to say that I wanted to become a nurse. I believe that in part it's a vocation, so that I think: this is mine. I see my job not only as a way to earn money, I want to be able to help people through it as well. I volunteer because various experiences have shown me that some women are pressured into terminating their pregnancy. They see no way that they could have the child because they get no help. We offer them that help. For me, both work and volunteering are a vocation. For me, that means that God has asked me to do what I do. And that I do it all the more willingly for that reason.

I particularly enjoy my work when I can see that people trust me and confide in me.

What I find stressful at work is when disagreements break out between colleagues that you can't solve, or when colleagues turn on each other. That doesn't happen very often, but now and again. Then I feel helpless.

If money didn't come into it, I would perhaps reduce my hours, but I would like to continue.

For my future career I hope that the work remains manageable. When there are so many residents that you can't look after each of them properly, then I find it very worrying, and I'm a little bit afraid of that happening. My dream, though it's one that I can't achieve for personal reasons, would be a responsible position on the administrative side, because that's where my talents lie.«

play a role.[84] For this mission she uses the term »call«[85], meaning something »which won't let you go«[86] and which summons you to »greater authenticity«.[87]

The five vocational steps – the »Spiritual career evolution«

What distinguishes her approach from Forster's – in addition to its being open to specific religious traditions – is its systematic treatment of vocation. She speaks of five ideal-typical steps in any »spiritual career evolution«[88] and cites in support one of her own studies, on people who have reached a point where they are able to integrate their faith with their (working) life. The first stage is »segmentation«, the separation of spirituality and everyday life. Here, faith is no more than »tradition« and has nothing to do with the rest of one's life.[89] Neal calls the second stage »spiritual crisis«: prompted by the impact of dramatic external events or of spiritual experiences, one starts to question one's life up to that point. The role played previously by work is just »not right« any longer, a feeling of uncertainty takes hold. This spiritual crisis can lead to a »Dark Night of the Soul« – Neal's third stage. This is a period of depression, during which even previous sources of spirituality need to be called into question and tested once more. The fourth stage Neal identifies is concerned with »right livelihood«. Here, a new perspective on life, or a new work-life balance, is attained. This new perspective, according to Neal, opens up in a »moment

---

84 Ibid., 24.

85 Ibid., 32.

86 Ibid., quoting Martha I. FINNEY.

87 Ibid., 25.

88 Ibid., 29.

89 ibid., 29f.

of grace«, and is often described by Christians and by followers of other religions as »receiving a call«[90]; the outcome is *sometimes* a job switch, even if that sometimes means accepting financial penalties. Neal calls the fifth and final stage »beneficial presence«. In this stage, the activity itself is no longer the most important thing, but what she calls »inner development and working with the spiritual world for the good of mankind«.[91] She is thinking here of retirement or sabbaticals, when people focus on simplifying their lives and the primary purpose of their work is »to raise their level of consciousness«.[92] These, then, are the five steps, though the author emphasizes that they are not to be understood as linear, nor are they necessarily chronologically sequential.[93]

A consciously syncretic concept

In her scheme of a »spiritual career evolution«, Neal seeks to describe an ideal-typical route to vocation »in today's secular world«.[94] Her aim is to set out a concept that is open-ended with respect to religion, although the route she depicts has distinct echoes of certain mystical concepts. Her fourth stage (»right livelihood«) – as Neal herself points out – is taken from the »Eightfold Path« of Buddhism, in which it represents the highest expression of moral virtue (the fifth part of the path).[95] However, she goes beyond Buddhism by augmenting »right livelihood« with

---

90 Ibid., 31.

91 Ibid.

92 Ibid.

93 Ibid., 32.

94 Ibid., 32.

95 Ian S. Markham/Christy Lohr (Ed.s.), A World Religions Reader, Malden et al. ⁵2009, 95.

the element of illumination, or enlightenment. This step reveals the influence of Christian mysticism, and specifically of the classical triad of purgation – illumination – unification (*purgatio – illuminatio – unio*).[96] The »spiritual crisis« and the »dark night of the soul« can be linked to purgation – which is all the more plausible because with the phrase »dark night of the soul« Neal is alluding to the early modern mystic Saint John of the Cross. The stage of »right livelihood«, with its »call«, evokes that of illumination. And the beneficial presence has certain parallels to the unification with the divine, although Neal uses the non-theistic term »spiritual world« and speaks of a kind of universal interconnectedness, expressed for example through prayer.

Syncretic echoes of specific religious traditions can also be found in the four »themes of calling«[97] that Neal sketches out on the basis of her research. She cites the Benedictine motto »Labor[ar]e e[s]t orare« (»to work is to pray«) as evidence that work offers a possible link to »something greater«.[98] And she draws on Christian and Buddhist traditions when she cites, as a sign of spiritually oriented management, not only the renunciation of the »attachment to ego« but also »humility«. The aim is »selfless service«, which can mean both service of business success and service of one's colleagues[99] – as a first step from »me« to »we«.[100] Ultimately, however, the task is bigger than that: it is about »making a difference«, about the responsibility »to implement change and leave the world a better place«.[101] At this point,

---

96 Cf. Heinrich Stirnimann, Unio-communio: Dimensionen mystischer Erfahrung, Bd. 2, Freiburg i. Üe. 1996, 192.

97 Neal, Creating (see note. 25), 25.

98 Ibid., 25f.

99 Ibid., 28.

100 Ibid., 27.

101 Ibid., 28.

Neal comes back to the individual's »gifts«, which she interprets in a broadly religious sense: people achieve something positive when they recognise »the divine« in these gifts and put them to the service of others, for example to help their spiritual development.[102] Ultimately, Neal's aim is not only to enable a new awareness of spirituality at work but also to promote a »global conscious shift«, as the bearers of which she identifies »conscious capitalists« und »social entrepreneurs«.[103]

Interim conclusions

Judi Neal's conception of vocation is formulated in an explicitly inter-faith and eclectic way. With its tendency towards »spiritualist fluidity«[104], it contrasts with the decidedly Christian theological determination of conceptions such as Dion Forster's. Neal's version reflects a growing »loosening and merging of concepts of transcendence« which sociologists of religion have identified as »a feature of the metamorphosis of religion in the modern period«.[105] Neal is thus consciously aligning herself with a contemporary trend.

If we leave aside for a moment this tendency towards conceptual fluidity or indeterminacy, then the similarities with the Protestant concepts of vocation outlined above are clear. Vocation is found or located in one's given talents; it is something that has objective existence; and it entails responsibilities in the sense of service towards others. Further similarities can be found in its relatively post-materialist orientation and in the explicit desire to contrib-

---

102 Ibid.
103 Ibid., XVI.
104 POLLACK/ROSTA, Religion (see note 31), 477.
105 Ibid., 475.

ute to global change, although for Neal this change begins with a new awareness of the »interconnectedness with all things«[106] and of the inadequacy of an exclusively materialist worldview.[107] In contrast, the Protestants Miller and Ewest also took account of objective factors such as the fairness of the economic system.

Here we can see the orientation towards mysticism in Neal's conception, which also finds expression in her ideal-typical model of vocational stages. The merit of this model lies in how it connects with the desire for authenticity and the experience of crises of meaning in life and in work, and in taking up the issue of work-life balance and emphasising the value of the *Vita passiva* as against any normative paradigm of activism. It addresses the possibility of career change more directly than Forster does.

The limitations of this concept become apparent at several points. Its consciously eclectic approach makes vocation seem almost arbitrary. Its orientation towards mysticism downplays the role of structural factors; just as in Forster's concept, the importance of educational processes in enabling the recognition of one's vocation is not mentioned. Moreover, this concept again reflects only the experience of people in business and of entrepreneurs, here extended to include *social entrepreneurs*. The experience of people with a much more restricted scope for decision-making, with fewer resources and lower levels of formal education, plays no part in this concept. What also strikes one about Neal's concept is that the path she describes to the »spiritual career« is almost exclusively a highly individual one, almost elitist in fact. Although she does also mention religious practices and institutions, such as regular attendance at mass, or convents and ashrams, as well as particular people who can help one on the path to spirituality (a meeting with Mother Theresa, for example), the impression

---

106 NEAL, Creating (see note 25), XV.
107 Ibid., 18.

which remains is that of a highly individualistic path (even if it is intended ultimately to lead to a »we«). This is consistent with the occupational reality and above all with the self-understanding of »decision makers«.[108] The South African Thabo Makgoba, however, has drawn attention to the cultural determination – and thus the narrowness – of such a view of what human beings are like.

4. »Equally relevant to everyone«? – Criteria and challenges for a contemporary discourse of vocation

Our voyage of discovery through the wide world of WPS has led us to one of its core points: the discourse on vocation/calling. The survey of both explicitly Christian and consciously interfaith concepts has revealed once more the full spectrum encompassed within WPS. It ranges across »religion« and »spirituality«, and seeks to bring the personal search for meaning, values and beliefs together with the world of work. Both of these aspects serve to make WPS relevant to the European context as well.

This applies in the first instance to the link between spirituality and work. Here in Germany, too, the expectation or requirement for our career to provide meaning is considerable, especially when the borders between »work« and »life« are dissolving. Employees increasingly see their careers as the locus for self-realisation – and this is something that employers know how to exploit. A focus on values and openness to diversity are becoming positives in the competitive environment. And this shows that in Germany, too, the relationship between spirituality and work is no longer a niche topic, but has long since become an issue rich with potential.

---

108 Nassehi points out how individualism is constituted or expresses itself in personal accountability for specific decisions (ARMIN NASSEHI, Soziologie. Zehn einführende Vorlesungen, Wiesbaden ²2011, 133ff.).

Allied to this, the relationship between spirituality and religion has acquired new significance. Although spirituality is not (yet?) as widespread as in the USA, the proportion of Germans who describe themselves as spiritual rather than religious is now over 17 percent.[109] This has consequences for the Church, too, when it speaks on issues of meaning, values and working life. It finds itself confronted with the challenge of formulating its stance less in terms of tradition and with a greater focus on experience, guided not so much by fixed certainties as by the spirit of exploration.

As regards the discourse of vocation, the relevant concepts from the WPS movement presented here demonstrate certain strengths and weaknesses. From these we can now derive in conclusion some *criteria* for a contemporary discourse of vocation.

1. A concept of vocation is useful and relevant if it starts from concrete experiences and needs. Among these is the need for meaning and authenticity; the joy of being able to apply one's gifts in one's life and in the service of others; but also, the experience of rupture and of failure.

2. A concept of vocation is inadequate if it reflects only the experience of privileged and well-educated entrepreneurs. And it is misleading if it suggests that biographical development can only be singular and linear. Not only in Christological terms, but empirically too, it is important to acknowledge that fragmentariness belongs to human existence.[110] The discourse of vocation is only useful and relevant if it connects with the experience of less privileged people as well.

3. It seems to make sense to expand the meaning of the term vocation beyond that of a singular, non-recurring and completely

---

109 HEINZ STREIB, Abgelehnte Religion. Spiritualität – und die Frage nach der verlorenen Dimension, in: DtPfBl 11/2016, 626–629, 628.

110 HENNING LUTHER, Religion und Alltag. Bausteine zu einer Praktischen Theologie des Subjekts, Stuttgart 1992, 160ff., especially 173.

unambiguous »call«. Although there is such a thing as an unambiguous recognition of one's vocation, Dirk Kaesler has rightly pointed out that alongside such »endogenous« certainties found or formed in the individual consciousness, the choice of one's career or occupation (and the same applies to other things such as voluntary work) is also influenced by other factors, namely »exogenous«, (»social«) and »situational« ones.[111] Among these are processes of education, labour market prospects and opportunity structures. Vocation has to be thought of as differentiated and also as subject to biographical dynamics. This is especially true in times of discontinuous employment patterns and lifelong learning. Not only »career switchers« but also »career starters»[112] must be taken into account.

4. This also represents a critique of any discourse of vocation which assumes the existence of a unique and singular »calling« for every person, which she or he simply has to find. This desire for clarity is understandable at a time of social and economic change and of external »insecurity«.[113] But it becomes problematic if it leads to a constricting pressure which equates it with a narrow search for identity, one which is insufficiently open to biographical and situational factors.[114] In the Reformation tradition, the significance of the discourse of vocation lies precisely in responding to specific situations with the »freedom and love« that God has given to the human race.[115] The emphasis here is not on an abstract

---

111 Dirk Kaesler, Wie finde ich meine Berufung? Warum es immer noch besser ist, Max Weber zu lesen als Tarot-Karten zu legen, Literaturkritik.de, September 2011, online: http://literaturkritik.de/public/rezension.php?rez_id=15890 (accessed: 8.2.2017).

112 Cf. ibid.

113 Cf. ibid.

114 Adorno nach Luther, Religion (see note 110), 171.

115 Wagner, Berufung (see note 66), 712. According to Wagner, this is precisely how the religious or universal vocation and the particular or inner vocation are linked (ibid.).

vocation, but on the productive application of one's talents and gifts in concrete situations. In cases of doubt, it is precisely in such situations that one's vocation can be found and experienced.

5. A significant aspect of the vocation discourse is the emphasis on the subjectivity of every human being. Vocation is about whatever »won't let you go«, or what makes possible one's individual experience of finding meaning. However, the exclusive focus on individualism can lead to a false reductionism. This is shown by intercultural comparisons, but also by consideration of the realities of working life: work can only succeed and make sense today as a form of »cooperative community undertaking«, which requires a corresponding »communicative work ethic«.[116]

6. The fact that these concepts of vocation place the search for meaning through work at their core is to be welcomed. This not only underlines the interconnectedness of all spheres of life but also places certain ethical expectations on behaviour in the worlds of work and business. But the idea of vocation needs to be extended beyond the world of work. If the Reformation concept of vocation applies to specific, concrete situations, then it potentially covers all spheres of life. They can all become »places of responsibility«.[117] And this means that a comprehensive concept of vocation is needed, one that encompasses voluntary work and family and caring duties as well. The topic of vocation is certainly not »equally relevant to everyone«.[118] But any concept of vocation *should always have the potential* to be relevant to everyone.

---

116 COUNCIL OF THE EVANGELICAL CHURCH IN GERMANY/RAT DER EKD (Ed.), Solidarität und Selbstbestimmung im Wandel der Arbeitswelt. Eine Denkschrift, Gütersloh 2015, 31.

117 DOUGLAS J. SCHUURMAN, Vocation. Discerning Our Callings in Life, Cambridge 2004, 26.

118 KAESLER, Berufung (see note 111).

Abbreviations

Cf.	confer, compare
Ed.(s)	editor(s)
EKD	Evangelische Kirche in Deutschland = Evangelical Church in Germany
DtPfBl	Deutsches Pfarrerblatt, Stuttgart 1, 1897ff.
FGLP	Forschungen zur Geschichte und Lehre des Protestantismus, München 1, 1928ff.
Ibid.	Ibidem, in the same book or article
MEW	Karl Marx/Friedrich Engels, Werke, Berlin 1, 1956-42,1983
QD	Quaestiones disputatae, Freiburg i. Br. et al., 1/1958ff.
RGG	Religion in Geschichte und Gegenwart, Tübingen, 4th edition 1998ff.
SI	Sozialwissenschaftliches Institut der EKD = Social Sciences Institute oft the Evangelical Church in Germany
WPS	Workplace spirituality
TRE	Theologische Realenzyklopädie, Berlin 1, 1976ff.
WA	Martin Luther, Werke (Weimarer Ausgabe), Weimar 1, 1883ff.

The Authors

Füser, Anika, M.A.:

Sociologist and educational psychologist, research associate at the Social Sciences Institute (SI) of the Evangelical Church in Germany (EKD), Hannover.

Schendel, Gunther, Dr. theol.:

Pastor, theologian and church historian, research associate at the Social Sciences Institute (SI) of the Evangelical Church in Germany (EKD).

Wegner, Gerhard, Prof. Dr. theol.:

Pastor, director of the Social Sciences Institute (SI) of the Evangelical Church in Germany (EKD), associate professor for Practical Theology at the Philipps Universität Marburg, chairman of Niedersächsischer Bund für freie Erwachsenenbildung e.V. / Lower Saxon League for Liberal Adult Education.